THEOLOGICAL ANTHROPOLOGY:
A GUIDE FOR THE PERPLEXED

THEOLOGICAL ANTHROPOLOGY: A GUIDE FOR THE PERPLEXED

MARC CORTEZ

t&t clark

Published by T&T Clark International
A Continuum Imprint
The Tower Building   80 Maiden Lane
11 York Road   Suite 704
London SE1 7NX   New York NY 10038

www.continuumbooks.com

British Library Cataloguing-in-Publication Data
A catalogue record for this book is available from the British Library

ISBN: 978-0-567-03431-1 (Hardback)
        978-0-567-03432-8 (Paperback)

Typeset by Newgen Imaging Systems Pvt Ltd, Chennai, India
Printed on and bound in Great Britain by CPI Antony Rowe,
Chippenham, Wiltshire

This book is dedicated to my girls

CONTENTS

Chapter 1: Introduction   1
Chapter 2: *Imago Dei*   14
Chapter 3: Sexuality   41
Chapter 4: Mind and Body   68
Chapter 5: Free Will   98
Chapter 6: Conclusion   131

Notes   141
Bibliography   156
Scripture Index   163
Author Index   165

INTRODUCTION

A cow is always simply a cow. It does not ask, "What is a cow? Who am I?" Only man asks such questions, and indeed clearly has to ask them about himself and his being. This is his question. His question follows him in hundreds of forms.[1]

Jürgen Moltmann

"What is man that you are mindful of him, the son of man that you care for him?" (Ps. 8.4). In raising this question, the psalmist participated in one of humanity's oldest tasks—understanding itself. Philosophers, theologians, and scientists from every age and tradition have pursued this question endlessly, producing myriad perspectives and answers. Yet we might well wonder why this is such a difficult question to answer. Of *course* we know what a human person is. *We* are human persons. Indeed, there seems to be nothing with which we are so intimately involved as our knowledge of what it means to be human. We experience "humanity" everyday in ourselves and in our relationships with the people around us. I might not be able to tell you exactly what a platypus is, but I know all about what it means to be human. As G. C. Berkouwer asked,

Who does not "know" man, whom we daily encounter, and the man that we ourselves are? Is not the problem of the "nature" of man an abstract problem, a strange, reflexive, obvious problem? Is not this "nature" experienced by all of us, in ourselves and in others, in countless relationships, in the heights of human happiness and the depths of grief? Who does not "know" man, whom we daily encounter, and the man that we ourselves are?[2]

Despite our intimate familiarity with being human, however, we continue to be plagued with uncertainty about what it *means* to be human. Rather than providing an answer to this anthropological query, modern society is characterized by an ever-growing uncertainty that it is even possible to offer such an answer. For many modern thinkers, there is no identifiable self constituting the "I" of the question. Instead, the "I" is a fragmented and continuously shifting compilation of experiences and relationships.[3] We are not only uncertain about our ability to answer the question of identity, "*Who* am I?" but we can also see a growing lack of confidence in our ability even to answer the question of essence, "*What* am I?" The modern era has witnessed a remarkable number of new scientific and philosophical disciplines dedicated to understanding the human. Yet none of these offers answers that are ultimately satisfying. Should we understand human persons as *Homo sapiens*, members of the animal kingdom distinguished by certain biological characteristics? Certainly; but, is that adequate? Would not most people affirm that the human person is somehow "more" than the sum of his or her biological characteristics? Even with the advent of the neurosciences and their remarkable ability to analyze the complex factors that comprise a person's cognitive and psychological processes, we still resist the notion that these really capture the essence of what it means to be human. Confidence that we really understand humanity remains elusive. Thus, the human person "keeps on slipping out of his own grasp and becomes more of a puzzle to himself, the more possible solutions he has available in the form of outlines of what human is. The more possible answers he has, the more he feels he is in a hall of a thousand mirrors and masks, the more unintelligible he is to himself."[4] Despite our intimate familiarity with being human, it would seem that there are mysterious depths to the human person that constantly evade us.

Yet the significant implications that attach to how we answer the anthropological question mean that the query cannot simply be avoided—issues such as genetic engineering, human cloning, artificial intelligence, and globalization as well as the challenges of racism, classism, and sexism. Responding to these existential issues adequately, however, is inseparable from who and what we understand ourselves to be. Our answers to the questions "*Who* am I?" and "*What* am I?" are intimately connected to the question of

"*How* ought I to be in the world?" In other words, theological anthropology can never be entirely descriptive. A description of human nature always both presumes and entails a prescription for human living. The *what/who* questions and the *how* question are inseparable.[5] Properly understood, then, anthropology is not just a theoretical pursuit for some abstract human "nature" that dwells only in philosophy textbooks. Indeed any attempt to discuss human "ontology"—for example, the body/soul relationship, the nature of "free will," and so on—sounds only distantly related to the pressing concerns of living humanly in the world. Yet we must understand that these "theoretical" discussions have a direct bearing on practical realities. As Christoph Schöbel rightly argues, "Ontology is not only a field of abstract philosophical speculation. The different ontologies come to expression in the decisions we make, in the experiences we cherish or abhor, in the lifestyles we adopt or reject."[6] Our "abstract" understanding of human nature is enfleshed in the everyday decisions that we make as we live out our humanity.

THE RISE OF MODERN THEOLOGICAL ANTHROPOLOGY

Theologians have always been interested in the key issues surrounding the nature of the human person. Thus, from the very beginning of Christian theology, we find Christian thinkers wrestling with such anthropological questions as the body–soul relationship, gender, free will, the purpose of human life, and the relationship of human persons to the rest of creation, among other things. Early thinkers such as Irenaeus, Gregory of Nyssa, Augustine, and Maximus, were keenly interested in such issues and their significance for the life and theology of the church. Nonetheless, we must also note that for most of these thinkers, anthropology was not an object of reflection in itself. With few exceptions, each addressed these anthropological questions as a subset of some other study (e.g., salvation, ecclesiology, eschatology).

The twentieth century, however, witnessed a surge of interest in theological anthropology as a significant theological doctrine in its own right. This resurgence has taken place for a number of different reasons. To some extent, it simply mirrors the growing interest in the human person that has taken place in society as a whole. The modern era has been marked by a decisive "turn toward the self" evidenced in much modern philosophy and art. This widespread focus on the "self" as the focal point of all experience and knowledge "could not but have an impact on theology."[7] At the same time, the twentieth century also witnessed the proliferation of scientific disciplines devoted to understanding the human person. The need for theological reflection on the data produced by these disciplines contributed to the growth of theological anthropology.

On a more pragmatic level, the rise of theological anthropology in the twentieth century matched a corresponding rise of several critical challenges that fostered a serious reconsideration of what it means to be human. The atrocities of World War I ended the liberal ideal of an enlightened and continually progressing humanity. Its sequel, World War II, with the holocaust and the advent of the nuclear age, raised its own questions about the mysterious, and often evil, depths of human nature. More recent developments have generated their own questions: the fears raised by a globalizing economy with the corresponding questions regarding economic justice and equality; concerns about the growing ecological crisis and questions regarding how human persons are related to the rest of the created world; the growing acceptance of different expressions and public displays of sexuality and questions about the relationship between sexuality, gender, and human nature; the continued success of modern science in explaining and exploring the nature of the physical universe and questions about the nature of the human soul and the relationship between determinism and free will. All of these, among others, raised awareness in the twentieth century that theologians needed to be actively engaged in thinking about what it means to be human.

Even more importantly, however, we should recognize that this anthropological resurgence has important theological roots based on a growing appreciation for the fact that a properly God-centered theology does not need to neglect the human in the process. The Protestant liberal theologians of the nineteenth century began the modern shift toward an increased theological concern for the human person. The way in which they did so, however, often made the human person the focal point of theological reflection. Reacting against this anthropocentric theology, more conservative theologians often developed theological systems that tended to neglect anthropology entirely. During the course of the twentieth century, however, a number of other key theologians—including Barth, Rahner, Tillich, von Balthasar, and Pannenberg—argued that a properly theocentric theology must still recognize the importance that God has placed on the human person in establishing humanity as the objects of his covenantal relationality and eschatological purposes.[8] In other words, theological anthropology takes the human person as an important object of theological reflection because the triune God has drawn the human person into the theological narrative and, consequently, has made a theological understanding of the human a necessary and vital aspect of the theological task.

WHAT IS THEOLOGICAL ANTHROPOLOGY?

In the modern age, then, anthropology has become an area of theological reflection in its own right. Indeed, theological anthropology can be defined briefly in just this way—theological reflection on the human person. It may be more helpful, however, if we unpack this definition somewhat. That theological anthropology is *theological* expresses one of its basic convictions—the human person can be fully understood only from a theological perspective. The creation of human persons, their status as beings made in the image of God, their fall into a sinful state, and their subsequent redemption and eschatological glorification, all of these are theological realities without which the human person is not fully comprehended. Indeed, from this perspective, the human person is always-already defined and determined by his relationship to God. Consequently, we must affirm, "The relation of man's nature to God is not something that is added to an already complete, self-enclosed, isolated nature; it is essential and constitutive for man's nature, and man cannot be understood apart from this relation."[9] For theological anthropology, then, true knowledge of the human person begins with the relationship between God and humans.

That theological anthropology begins with the divine–human relationship, however, also means that it must begin with the person and work of Jesus Christ. As the one who is both fully human and fully divine, the true image of God, the redeemer of humanity, and the teleological focus of all creation, the mystery of humanity finds its most complete manifestation in Jesus. As Karl Barth famously declared, "The nature of the man Jesus alone is the key to the problem of human nature."[10] Theological anthropology, then, should begin its understanding of the human person by looking first to see how Jesus Christ manifests true humanity. From this vantage point we will be better positioned to understand the nature of our own humanity as we find it in this broken world. As we will see throughout this study, the Christological orientation of theological anthropology has implications for understanding nearly every aspect of human existence.

We must also affirm, however, that theological anthropology is about *anthropology*. The basic task of theological anthropology is to understand the human person. This does not mean that theological anthropology pursues knowledge of some abstract human nature removed from the realities of life; rather, theological anthropology seeks knowledge of the human person as he or she actually exists in the world. As such, the human person is available for study from a variety of perspectives, each of which offers important insights into various aspects of human existence. A growing number of thinkers and research in various fields (e.g., cultural anthropology, philosophy of mind, psychology, sociology, neuroscience) are hard at work trying to shed some light on what it means to be human. As an anthropological discipline, theological anthropology should be involved in constant dialogue with these other disciplines, seeking to understand what they have to offer for understanding humanity and allowing its own insights and conclusions to be stretched and reshaped when necessary by the data they produce. Indeed, theological anthropology has always participated in such dialogue with the surrounding culture based on its conviction that, if God is the creator of all reality, we should not reject truth wherever it might be found. The modern situation differs only in the range and complexity of available dialogue partners.

At the same time, however, theological anthropology cannot simply adopt whatever results are produced by these other anthropological disciplines. Indeed, in many ways, theological anthropology entails the conviction that the perspectives offered by nontheological anthropologies are inherently limited, possibly even flawed. If the true reality of what it means to be human is revealed only as we understand the human person in relationship to God, and more specifically as we view the human person through the person and work of Jesus Christ, then any attempt to understand humanity in abstraction from this theological reality is necessarily limited and ultimately inadequate. This does not mean that the insights provided by nontheological anthropologies are unimportant. Indeed, in many ways they are vital for a full understanding of human existence. Although theological anthropology lays claim to being the only proper starting point for understanding human persons adequately, it does not claim to be able to tell us everything that we need to know about the human person. Instead theological anthropology recognizes its dependence on the other anthropological disciplines for understanding much that is important about the psychology, sociology, and ontology of the human person. Thus, theological anthropology recognizes these other disciplines as legitimate partners in the process while insisting on its right to evaluate and interpret the data provided by these nontheological disciplines from its own perspective. Theologians "may not undiscriminatingly accept the data provided by a nontheological anthropology and make these the basis for their own work."[11] Instead, theological anthropology seeks to find in this data that which is useful in explicating what it means to be human, remaining free to reshape those conclusions according to its "particular angle of vision"[12] when necessary. Properly understood, then, theological anthropology is that area of Christian reflection that seeks to understand the mystery of humanity by reflecting theologically—and, thus, Christologically—on the human person in constant and critical dialogue with the other anthropological disciplines.

THE CONTEMPORARY CHALLENGE OF THEOLOGICAL ANTHROPOLOGY

We should also recognize that any theological anthropology faces a number of significant challenges. Although none of these can be eliminated—indeed, some of them are part and parcel of why theological anthropology is important—identifying and understanding them should at least make us aware of the potential pitfalls they entail.

The first difficulty of any anthropological study is that the object of study is *ourselves*. Unlike other disciplines where we can pretend to some form of objectivity in seeking to analyze the data under consideration, with anthropology the subjective nature of our inquiry is unavoidable. "No man can abstract himself from his own nature, and it is precisely this fact which gives such an existential character to every judgment about 'man' and to every view of man's nature."[13] We must be constantly aware of the fact that our anthropological conclusions will often be shaped more by our own experiences and preconceptions than by the data under consideration. Issues such as gender, race, and class are objects of inquiry at the same time that one's gender, race, and class significantly shape the conclusions we reach. Thus, any anthropologian faces the temptation of creating "human nature" in his or her image. This does not mean that we have to abandon the attempt as lapsing necessarily into a solipsistic relativism, but it does mean that we should apply some "hermeneutic of suspicion" to our anthropological conclusions as well as those of others.

Theological anthropology is also challenging because it is a task that is never complete; indeed, it is a task that *cannot* be completed. Although we will often speak of theological anthropology as trying to "understand" the human person, we must acknowledge that there is a sense in which this will never be fully accomplished. What it means to be human is ultimately "hidden with Christ in God" (Col. 3.3) and is not something that can be fully "acquired" and "grasped" by us. As John declares, "what we will be has not yet appeared; but we know that when he appears we shall be like him, because we shall see him as he is" (1 Jn 3.2). We must affirm that in the incarnation Jesus has already come as the true human who reveals true humanity to us. This is the true and certain foundation for theological reflection on the human person. At the same time, however, we must recognize that even this revelation of humanity is not entirely complete. We still await the eschatological realization of God's full purposes for humanity. Although we see in Jesus what it means for a truly human person to live a God-oriented and Spirit-directed life, we have yet to see what it looks like when the people of God as a community live transformed lives in the midst of a redeemed and sin-free world. Theological anthropology's knowledge of the human, then, is always bounded and chastened by the knowledge that it awaits this eschatological fulfillment.

At the same time, theological anthropology's task is never complete because of the remarkable ability that humans have for creating new problems and raising new questions that must be understood and addressed in every age. As theological anthropology seeks to understand human persons as they actually are in the world, it must continuously face the challenging questions of living humanly in a broken world. In this sense, "being human" is a task that every generation is called to understand anew; in every age, theological anthropology must begin again.

Another challenge that one encounters in theological anthropology is the lack of explicit biblical and confessional data with respect to some of the most fundamental anthropological questions. What does it mean for a human person to have a "free will?" Although the Bible routinely assumes that human persons are in fact "free," one looks in vain for any biblical discussion of what this means. Similarly, the Bible regularly uses terms such as "body," "soul," and "spirit" to describe the human person, and yet their use is remarkably fluid in the biblical texts, leaving room for significant ambiguity in understanding their precise relationship. This problem recurs with most of the major issues in theological anthropology. This does not mean that the Bible is unconcerned with the nature of the human; such questions are pivotal in the biblical portrayal of redemption. However, the Bible does seem relatively unconcerned with addressing these issues with the kind of precision that is often necessary to address the difficult questions involved in theological anthropology. Thus, theologians are seldom able to cite clear biblical texts in support of particular positions; instead, the anthropologian will usually need to develop larger frameworks for understanding the human person within which more particular formulations can function and their adequacy tested. We will see this at play several times in this book.

One final problem that we encounter in theological anthropology is the problem of sin. There are actually two related challenges here. The first is that theological anthropology works with "broken" data. Somewhat like the archeologist who tries to piece together the truth of an event from broken and often confusing data, the theologian must look at the broken reality of human lives and human communities—trying to piece together an understanding of it means to be truly human. Even with the revelation of true humanity that we find in Christ, we are still faced with the challenge of understanding how that revelation applies to humanity as a whole, a task made daunting by the reality of human sin. This leads to the second challenge. Given the sinful state of humanity, we might be tempted to be satisfied with an account of "true humanity" as an abstract concept separate from the hard realities of a broken world. Although we will see that knowledge of prototypical humanity (i.e., human persons at creation) and eschatological humanity (i.e., humanity's *end* or *goal*) should continually inform our understanding of humanity at every step, each can become abstract concepts if left isolated from humanity as we actually experience it. "It is well to remember . . . that we are not dealing with an abstract *idea* of man, but with actual man. Reflection that thinks it can ignore the darker aspects of man's nature is occupied with an abstraction and will never acquire the right view of the actual problems of man's life."[14] To the extent that we understand the importance of addressing the *how* question as well as the *what* and the *who* of anthropology, we must engage humanity as we really find it, as well as what we believe it can and ought to be.

THE ISSUES IN CONTEMPORARY
THEOLOGICAL ANTHROPOLOGY

Now that we have a better understanding of what theological anthropology is and some of the important challenges that it faces, we can turn our attention to the key issues theological anthropology seeks to address. Without question, the two central issues of theological anthropology traditionally have been understanding the *imago Dei* and sin. The first statement that the Bible makes about human persons declares the divine intent to create them in his "image and likeness." Unsurprisingly, then, this statement is often taken as the starting point of theological anthropology and the central concept in understanding what it means to be human as God intended. Immediately after this creation story, however, the biblical narratives record humanity's fall into sin. With this comes a ream of questions about the nature of sin and its impact on the *imago Dei*, on human nature, and community in general. These two concepts, then, have traditionally served as the framework within which theologians discuss the original nature and purpose of humanity as well as the loss of this original state through the fall into sin.

In addition to these two, quite a number of other issues are also associated with theological anthropology. Some of those issues are inseparable from other areas of Christian doctrine. The fundamental anthropological significance of Jesus Christ, the role of the Spirit in human life, the story of redemption and its eschatological conclusion, all of these take anthropology far afield and demonstrate its inseparable relationship with all areas of Christian doctrine.

Other issues more specific to theological anthropology include the following:

- When and how were humans created? How do different creation stories influence our understanding of what it means to be human?
- What is the relationship between human persons and the rest of creation? How "unique" are humans in creation? How does this affect our appreciation for the "dignity" of the human person?
- Why were humans created male and female? What is the significance of human sexuality for understanding humanity? How should this play out in our understanding of marriage, family, and sexual ethics?
- Of what are human persons comprised? Are we basically physical beings, spiritual beings, some combination of the two, or something else entirely? In what ways does our answer to this question affect how humans should live in the world?
- Do human persons have "free will"? What exactly does this mean and what is its significance for understanding, among other things, salvation, moral responsibility, and relationality?
- What exactly is "personhood" and why is it important for understanding humanity? What does it mean to be a "self"? How is personal identity formed and sustained?
- How do interpersonal relationships and community inform what it means to be human? How do we balance the individual and corporate aspects of humanity?
- How important is "race" to being human? Is it an essential aspect of humanity or is it a cultural creation?
- How do economic and class issues relate to humanity? Is work an essential aspect of being human, or only something that we do to serve other purposes?

Although these are some of the major issues with which contemporary anthropology must be concerned, the list could be extended almost indefinitely to encompass the entire range of questions that arise in the process of understanding human persons. Given the mystery and complexity of humanity, we should expect nothing less.

Because all of these issues are important to theological anthropology, any of them would have served well as topics for the remaining chapters in this book. Unfortunately, choices must always be made and issues excluded. So, I have selected four of these issues for further consideration: the *imago Dei*, human sexuality, human constitution (i.e., the body/soul relationship), and free will. The first of these, the *imago Dei*, is such a central aspect of most theological anthropologies that it really cannot be avoided in any adequate discussion. Chapter 2, then, will address the *imago Dei* and the important role that it plays as a central concept of most theological anthropologies. Here we will survey a number of different proposals for understanding the *imago Dei* and how it relates to being human. I will then argue for a way of bringing together two of those proposals to understand the human person as imaging God by manifesting his personal presence in creation. This will serve to provide us with an important theological framework for understanding the human person that will guide the other discussions.

In Chapter 3, we will turn our attention to human sexuality. This topic is ripe for discussion for at least two reasons. First, like the *imago Dei*, human sexuality plays a prominent role in the creation narratives. Indeed, the "male and female" of the human person is arguably a more central feature of Genesis 1–2 than the *imago Dei* itself. Second, few issues in theological anthropology are more hotly debated today and more complex than those involving human sexuality. Taking some time to think through those issues will be time well spent. Thus, in this chapter, we will consider different ways in which people have tried to understand the nature of human sexuality from both secular and theological perspectives. In the process, we will see that the theological purpose of human sexuality is most properly understood when it is understood as that which grounds human relationality and, in this way, provides an important basis for imaging God's personal presence.

Chapter 4 will focus on the constitution of the human person. Although Christian theologians have traditionally espoused some form of dualism—that is, that human persons comprise some combination of a soul-substance and a body-substance—the rise of the modern sciences and a growing appreciation for the physical underpinnings of human behavior have contributed to the growth of physicalism, that is, that human persons are entirely physical beings—as a way of understanding human ontology. The debate between these two perspectives has grown in intensity in recent years, making this an important area of consideration for theological anthropology. In this chapter, then, we will try to understand some of the key issues involved in this debate. Rather than argue for the superiority of one view over the other, however, this chapter will draw on the theological framework developed in our discussion of the *imago Dei*, to argue that the precise theory that we adopt in understanding human ontology is less important than making sure that we are framing the question properly. I do not want to downplay the importance of this vital debate, but I will argue that we need to make sure that we have located the debate properly.

The last of our issues, free will, will be the topic of Chapter 5. Perhaps no other issue in theological anthropology has been the source of such sustained debate as that of free will. Indeed, from the time of the early church to date, theologians have waged a constant war of words, and sometimes worse, over this issue. Furthermore, theologians are not alone. Free will remains a contentious issue for contemporary philosophers and scientists as well. Given the perennial nature of this debate, it should come as no surprise that this chapter will not offer a definitive resolution. Indeed, given the complexity of the problem and myriad implications that any proposed solution entails, one wonders whether a definitive resolution is even possible. Our focus in this chapter, then, will again be on understanding the major proposals on the table and then drawing on our theological framework for providing an adequate way of working through the issues. Once again we will see that the *manner* in which we approach the problem will be at least as important, if not more so, than the *matter* of any particular conclusion.

Once again we must realize that these four issues are only some of the key challenges facing contemporary anthropology. Nonetheless, they constitute four of the most important and contentious problems and are well worth our attention. At the same time, they provide us the opportunity for developing a way of doing theological anthropology that should serve as a model for engaging other issues as well. The focus of this book, then, will not be as much on offering definitive conclusions as on modeling a way of thinking theologically about the human person.

CHAPTER 2

IMAGO DEI

Thus far to try thee, Adam, I was pleased;
And find thee knowing, not of beasts alone,
Which thou has rightly named, but of thyself;
Expressing well the spirit within thee free,
My image not imparted to the brute,
Whose fellowship therefore unmeet for thee,
Good reason was thou freely should'st dislike:
And be so minded still. I, ere thou spak'st,
Knew it not good for Man to be alone;
And no such company as then thou saw'st
Intended thee; for trial only brought,
To see how thou could'st judge of fit and meet.
What next I bring shall please thee, be assure;
They likeness, they fit help, they other self

Milton, Paradise Lost, *7.437–50*

At the very beginning of the biblical narrative, we encounter one of the more audacious claims in the Bible: "God created man in his own image, in the image of God he created him; male and female he created them" (Gen. 1.27). Many of us have, perhaps, grown so comfortable with this verse and the claims that it makes for the nature and identity of human persons that we no longer recognize the fabulous nature of this assertion.[1] At the beginning of a work founded on the belief in an invisible God who cannot be depicted by images and who transcends human understanding, God declares his intent to image himself in finite, physical, and imperfect human beings.

Such a juxtaposition of the human and the divine in one theological assertion opens the door to a fundamental reorientation of each. Consequently, this statement has been understood by many theologians to stand at the very center of a properly Christian concept of what it means to be human, and the starting point of theological anthropology.

Given the central role that this concept has played, it is surprising to discover that the *imago Dei* actually occurs rather infrequently in the Bible. Indeed, after its initial use in the creation account, there are only two other direct references to the image in the Old Testament (OT; Gen. 5.1; 9.6). Although we find a few more references in the New Testament (NT; 1 Cor. 11.7; 2 Cor. 3.18; 2 Cor. 4.4; Eph. 4.24; Col. 1.15; Jas 3.9), that still amounts to a relatively small number of direct references to a concept that is considered by many to be "the most distinctive feature of the biblical understanding of man."[2] The relative scarcity of biblical material regarding the *imago* might lead some to wonder if it should continue to play such a central role in theological anthropology. A narrow focus on these direct references, however, neglects the important ways in which the concept of the *imago Dei* underlies and informs other biblical passages (e.g., Ps. 8.4–6). Thus, even when the *imago Dei* is not explicitly stated, it is frequently assumed.

Precisely how we understand the nature of this affirmation, however, has been the subject of intense debate throughout the centuries. As we will see, the biblical text is sufficiently ambiguous as to allow for a variety of different interpretations. Sorting through the biblical and extra-biblical data that inform these discussions can be daunting. Interpreters also face the challenges produced by their cultural location. All cultures have their own concept of what it most fundamentally means to be human. Because the *imago* stands at the center of many Christian conceptions of the human, it invariably enters into dialogue with and is significantly influenced by these other anthropologies. Indeed, as Edward Curtis has observed, "the interpretation of the image of God has often reflected the *Zeitgeist* and has followed whatever emphasis happened to be current in psychology, or philosophy, or sociology, or theology."[3] Our task, then, is to be aware of these challenges even as we strive to gain a better understanding of what it means to affirm that human beings are made in the image of God.

THE IMAGE OF GOD DEBATE: CONSENSUS AND DISAGREEMENT

a. Areas of general consensus

As we will see, precisely what this assertion means is hotly contested. Nonetheless, I think it will be helpful for us to note a few areas on which scholars are in general agreement.

To "image" God means to "reflect" God in creation. There is little debate that the basic idea of the image denotes that human persons "reflect" the divine reality in some way. The key terms—*selem* and *demut* in the OT, and *eikon* in the NT—all refer to the idea that some object reflects or resembles another in some way. This resemblance could take different forms—visual (e.g., Ezek. 1.5, 10, 13), audible (Isa. 13.4), or structural (2 Kgs 16.10)—and could indicate a resemblance that is a mere "shadow" of the corresponding reality (e.g., Ps. 39.6), or a much closer connection in which the image is understood to represent the presence of the corresponding reality in some way (e.g., Dan. 3). Throughout, however, the basic idea of the image as a "reflection" of some other object holds. The real debate, as we will see, begins when we try to explain more precisely what is reflected, where this is reflected in humanity, and how this reflection actually takes place.

"Image" and "likeness" are largely or entirely synonymous. Many patristic and medieval exegetes argued that there was an important theological distinction intended by the use of *selem* and *demut* in Genesis 1:27–28.[4] Contemporary exegetes, however, agree that these two terms are largely synonymous and that we should not read any strong distinction into their use in this text.[5]

The image of God includes all human persons. We also find virtual unanimity on the fact that all human persons—regardless of gender, race, or status—are made in the image of God. Some theologians in church history have argued that males alone were in the image of God, but scholars are now united in rejecting this interpretation. The Bible clearly affirms that both males and females are in the image of God (Gen. 1.27) and uses this as the basis for treating all human persons with dignity (Gen. 9.6; Jas 3.9).

Sin has affected the image in some way. This seems amply supported by the emphasis throughout the Bible on the pervasively depraved nature of human existence (Ps. 14.1–3; Rom. 3.23) and the consistent testimony of the NT that the image stands in need of renewal and restoration (Eph. 4.22–24; Col. 3.10). Despite this general agreement, the precise nature of this impact varies significantly depending on the particular view of the image that is in operation.

The image in the New Testament is a Christological concept. The clear testimony of the OT is that all human persons are made in the image of God. The NT authors continue this tradition (1 Cor. 11.7; Jas 3.9), but at the same time the NT also makes a fundamental shift in its understanding of the image. In the NT, the focus lies not on humans in general as the image of God but on Jesus Christ as the one who is the true *eikon* of God. Thus, Paul focuses primarily on Jesus Christ as the true image (2 Cor. 4.4; cf. Heb. 1.3), who makes the invisible God visible in creation (Col. 1.15). As one who was without sin (Heb. 4.15), Jesus is also the only true and unblemished *eikon*. Using slightly different language, the author of Hebrews expresses a similar concept in identifying Christ as the "exact representation" of the divine nature. Indeed, in the NT, the divine intent for human persons from the very beginning was not that they might be in the "image of God," but, surprisingly, that they might be "conformed to the image of his son" (Rom. 8.29; cf. 1 Cor. 15.49). Therefore, for the NT, the *imago Dei* is an inherently Christological concept.

The image of God is teleological. Finally, most thinkers affirm that the image is not an entirely static concept; instead, they view it as developing toward something—it has a teleological dimension. Thus, as we have seen, Paul portrays the image as something that is being "transformed" (2 Cor. 3.18) and "renewed" (Col. 3.10) in human persons as they are drawn ever closer to the person of Christ. For many theologians, this teleological element is a result of sin. That is, humans were fully in the image of God at creation, but that image was lost or marred after the Fall and stands in need of restoration. For other theologians, particularly those in the Eastern Orthodox tradition, the teleological dynamic of the image has been there from the beginning. Adam and Eve themselves were created with the intention that they would grow toward the image, who is Christ. Humans were thus "predestined to become conformed to the likeness of his son" (Rom. 8.29) from creation. Either way, theologians largely agree that the image of God in humans is a work in progress. It is moving toward its Christological goal, its *telos*.

b. The shape of the debate

Despite this broad consensus on a number of important issues, the question of the *imago Dei* remains contentious. At least four proposals vie for our attention.

The structural image

The most prevalent way of understanding the image of God throughout history has been in terms of some capacity or a set of capacities constitutive of being human that reflects the divine being in some way. The most common of such approaches identifies the *imago* as humanity's capacity for rational thought.[6] Thus, humans image a rational and wise God in their capacity for rational and wise thought. This was the predominant view in the early church and (at least) through the middle ages.[7] Although rationality is the capacity most often referred to by proponents of the structural approach, a number of other capacities have been suggested as denoting the primary distinguishing feature of the human person (e.g., symbolic reasoning, self-determination, moral agency, self-transcendence).[8] In every case, the structural view posits that the *imago* involves something essential to the nature of the human person, some capacity or set of capacities that characterize what the human person *is*.

Proponents of the structural approach typically rely on two key strategies to support their argument. The first involves an argument from human uniqueness. On this approach, proponents first identify the *imago* as something that sets human persons apart from the rest of creation. According to the creation narratives, only humans are made in the image of God. Thus, the *imago* should be that which makes humans different from other animals. The key task, then, is to determine what capacity (or capacities) sets the human person apart from other animals. The second approach moves in a vertical rather than a horizontal direction. This argument looks for capacities of the human person that have parallels in the divine being. For example, such thinkers argue that God clearly has the capacity for rational thought; so, it seems reasonable to conclude that a being who images God will also have the capacity for rational thought. This does not necessarily mean that human rationality is precisely the same as divine rationality; but they contend that there is at least an analogical relationship that supports the conclusion.

As the structural approach identifies the *imago Dei* as an essential aspect of the human person, a part of human nature, proponents of the structural approach typically argue that the human person retains the *imago Dei* even after the fall. Those arguing from this perspective will contend, for example, that humanity retains the capacity for rational thought after the fall, while typically affirming that sinful humans will always exercise this creaturely capacity in sinful ways.

Despite its historical influence most contemporary thinkers have rejected the structural approach as an adequate way of understanding the image. The most glaring weakness of the approach is its lack of exegetical support. One looks in vain for any clear (or even implicit) biblical link between the *imago* and some essential attribute of the human person. Lacking this, it becomes all too easy to identify the *imago* with the reigning cultural conception of what separates humans from other animals. Barth speaks for many by concluding, "[I]t is obvious that their authors merely found the concept in the text and then proceeded to pure invention in accordance with the requirement of contemporary anthropology."[9]

Another concern has to do with the way in which this approach often relies on identifying that which is unique to human persons, distinguishing them from the rest of creation. Such an approach, however, simply will not do for at least two reasons. First, although only humans are explicitly said to be in the image of God, other biblical texts make it clear that creation as a whole plays a similar imaging role. According to the psalmist, "The heavens declare the glory of God; the skies proclaim the works of his hand" (Ps. 19.1). In the NT, Paul declares that "God's invisible attributes have been clearly seen, being understood from what has been made" (Rom. 1.19). Regardless of one's position on the viability of natural theology, it seems clear that the biblical authors understood that all of creation images (i.e., "reflects") God. It is, of course, entirely possible that there are important differences in the way that humans image God in comparison to the rest of creation, differences that may explain why humans alone are called *imago Dei* beings in the creation narrative; but the fact that imaging God is common to all of creation should caution us about assuming too quickly that the *imago* will sharply distinguish humans from the rest of creation.

A second reason that this approach is unsatisfactory, however, is the growing realization that many of the things we once thought distinguished humans from the rest of creation are, in fact, shared with other creatures as well.[10] Indeed, it would be relatively easy to work through each of the proposed structural capacities and identify ways in which very similar sets of capacities can be found in other animals.[11] Again, there may still be ways in which humans are importantly different than animals with regard to each of these, but this should prevent us from assuming too quickly that certain characteristics of human persons are in fact unique in creation.

Yet another problem has to do with any attempt to define what it means to be human in terms of essential capacities or faculties. This will again not work for at least two related reasons. First, it is nearly impossible to find a structural capacity that applies to all human beings. The capacity for rational thought would not seem to apply to infants, many disabled people, or even normally functioning human adults who are temporarily unconscious. Of course, we could explain that what we mean by "capacity for rational thought" is that the individual in question would be rational if everything were fully developed and functioning properly. This definition only appears to succeed, however, by moving to such a high level of abstraction that it provides little, if any, help for understanding the concrete realities of human life. Thus, it would seem that any structural definition of the *imago* runs the risk of excluding certain categories of human beings from its definition of humanity.

This leads to the second consequence of this approach. What do we do with people who do not seem to exhibit those capacities? As a recent statement by a study group of the World Council of Churches warns, we must beware "the unconscious assumption, which pervades many of our cultures, that only a 'perfect' person can reflect fully the image of God – where 'perfect' means to be successful, attractive, young and not disabled."[12] Such a conclusion can only have disastrous consequences for our ability to appreciate the full personhood and dignity of all human beings.

Structural approaches can also be criticized for developing their perspective in highly individualistic terms. To the extent that the *imago* is understood as a capacity possessed and expressed by individual human persons (e.g., rationality), it fails to recognize that the emphasis in Genesis 1.26–28 is on humanity as a collective whole. Although we do not need to deny that the *imago* has application to particular individuals (Gen. 9.6; Jas 3.9), we should recognize that the emphasis in the creation narratives is on humanity as a whole as that which images God.[13]

Finally, the structural approach often emphasizes human capacities in rather disembodied ways. Thus, some proponents have argued that the body was not a proper part of the image of God because only the immaterial part of the person, the soul, directly images God. Yet once again we must recognize that the biblical narratives make no such distinction. Instead, Genesis 1.26–28 simply identifies human persons, presumably whole and embodied human persons, as imaging God. Looking to the subsequent reference in Genesis 5.1–3, Seth was presumably in the image of his father as a whole person as well. This disembodied understanding of the *imago* is not only without biblical support, but it is also inherently reductionistic. Although rationality is an important dimension of human life, human persons are certainly more than their rational (or volitional, spiritual, etc.) capacities alone. Indeed, human rationality itself cannot be understood in isolation from the relationships, cultural practices, biological conditions, and affective dimensions of the human person.[14] Each of the candidates for a structural understanding of the human person likewise struggles from a tendency to reduce the human person to one limited, albeit important, dimension.

For a variety of reasons, then, the structural approach fails to satisfy as an account of the image of God.

The functional image

A second approach argues that the *imago Dei* is something that human persons *do*, rather than something that human persons *are*. The image is a function of the human person (or the human community) and not a structure of the human person's being.[15] This functional understanding rests largely on two arguments.

The first argument considers the meaning of the *imago Dei* as it was used in other cultures of the ancient near east. The idea of a human person being "in the image" of a divine being was hardly unique to Israel. Indeed, it was well known in both Mesopotamia and Egypt. In those contexts, "image of God" referred to the fact that some humans, typically a kingly figure, were the official representatives of a divine being. This could either be because this person was understood to be an actual incarnation of some divine being (Egypt), or simply because he was viewed as a divinely appointed and empowered representative (Mesopotamia). In either case, the person served as a divine representative specifically for the purpose of exercising dominion. This cultural background is then used to provide more specificity to the meaning of the concept in the creation narratives. As beings made in the image of God, the human person "reflects" the divine reality by serving as God's representative rulers in the created realm. The main point of differentiation between the biblical concept and its use in surrounding cultures, then, is that the Bible declares all humans to be *imago Dei*.

This cultural argument is often buttressed with a second argument, one based on the close juxtaposition of "in our image" and "let them rule" in Genesis 1.26. According to some scholars, the latter phrase should be understood as a definition of the former, that is, the image of God is simply the exercise of dominion. Most scholars recognize, however, that mere juxtaposition is insufficient to establish identity. Instead, these thinkers argue that a better approach is to understand the latter as a result of the former, that is, humans exercise dominion *because* they represent God in the world. Regardless, the conclusion that these thinkers draw is that there is an intimate relationship between these two concepts such that the functional *imago* comes to be understood as "representative dominion."[16]

On the functional approach, the image of God remains in humanity after the fall but only in a twisted sense. Humans continue to serve as God's representative stewards over creation, but as sinful beings we have twisted this function so that it becomes hierarchical domination and oppression rather than stewardship as a manifestation of God's glory.

Unlike the structural approach, the functional approach develops its understanding of the *imago* largely on the basis of explicitly exegetical concerns. Indeed, this approach enjoys strong support from most contemporary biblical scholars. Nonetheless, the functional approach is not without its own critics. The first concern that many have about this approach is its dependence on extra-biblical sources and the corresponding assumption that the "image of God" must mean the same thing in Genesis as it does in other ancient texts. We need to be very careful about simply assuming that the ideas and practices of the surrounding cultures must provide the interpretive content of biblical ideas and practices. Indeed, we must be sensitive to the distinctive culture of ancient Israel and, more important, the distinctive theological framework of the OT, in understanding these texts. The fact of the matter is that the OT simply makes no attempt to link the image of God to the representative rulership of its kings, and it clearly develops its understanding of the image of God in markedly different ways (e.g., extending it to all persons and not just the kings). We should be careful, then, about imposing foreign ideas on the biblical texts.

At the same time, we should recognize that the biblical texts were not written in isolation from their cultural context, and our understanding of the terms that they use should be informed by that context. The fact that the author of Genesis uses words such as *selem* and *demut* without definition or explanation does point to an expectation that the readers would be able to draw on their cultural–linguistic resources to understand their meaning and, consequently, that we should be able to do likewise. Thus, while being sensitive to ways in which the particular cultural and theological perspectives of ancient Israel may have modified and reshaped the concepts they share with their broader culture, we can and should utilize these broader contexts in understanding the biblical texts.

A second argument that can be raised against the functional approach is that it suffers from an overly narrow focus on the first chapter of Genesis in determining the meaning of the *imago Dei*. It thus fails to consider the function of that passage within the narrative flow of Genesis and, indeed, the rest of the canon. Even though we should recognize the important differences between the two creation accounts, we must also understand the significance of their canonical location in immediate proximity to one another. Although the second chapter of Genesis makes no explicit reference to the *imago Dei*, it continues the Genesis account of humanity's creation and raises a number of important themes that should be taken into consideration. For example, in Genesis 2 we see human persons exercising some form of "rule" over creation; entering into meaningful relationships with God, one another, and the rest of creation; existing as a being that shares a common creaturehood with other animals, yet standing apart from other creatures in important ways; being summoned into a morally accountable position before God; and, finally, coming together as male and female as an important part of completing what God intended for human persons. Taking the two chapters together forces us to realize that although the first chapter declares God's creation of humanity to be good, the second indicates that Adam as a individual, male human lacks something that was fulfilled only by the creation of another human person, a female, with whom he could enter into a meaningful, human relationship. A narrow focus on the first chapter alone, then, may cause us to miss something important being expressed in the overall flow of the narrative. Similarly, an exclusive focus on the meaning of "in the image" in Genesis could cause us to miss the fundamental reorientation of the concept that we encounter in the NT. However we understand the image in Genesis 1.26–28, we must do so in such a way that it finds its ultimate fulfillment in Jesus Christ and its final manifestation in the eschatological union of Christ and his church. The proper interpretive context of Genesis 1.27–28, then, is not just Genesis 1 alone but the entire scope of the narrative that it initiates.

Therefore, although the functional approach to the image contains some real insights that we may well want to retain, we must also recognize some important limitations.

The relational image

Many theologians have found themselves dissatisfied with either the structural or functional approaches.[17] They contend that the true meaning of the *imago* is to be found in "relations."[18] That is, human persons are fundamentally relational beings—related to God, to other humans, and to creation—and it is this relationality that truly images a God who is himself a relational being. The fundamentally relational nature of human persons is seen most clearly in the male–female differentiation of humanity. By constituting human persons as sexually distinct, God created in humanity an essential relationality that mirrors the relationality inherent in the Trinity itself. As Barth declares, "Man is created by God in correspondence with this relationship and differentiation in God Himself: created as a Thou that can be addressed by God but also an I responsible to God; in the relationship of man and woman in which man is a Thou to his fellow and therefore himself an I in responsibility to this claim."[19]

Supporters of the relational *imago* appeal to at least three exegetical bases for their approach. First, some argue for the significance of the divine plural in this context. God's reference to himself in the plural, "Let us," for these thinkers, at least hints at the relationality inherent in the three persons of the godhead. Others have modified this proposal slightly, arguing that these plural pronouns do not make a direct reference to the Trinitarian nature of God, but they do indicate a "something more" in the unity of the divine being, a "fullness" that transcends mere solitariness. Consequently, we would expect that any creature created to image that divine reality would do so in a similarly relational manner. This argument has not received much support among biblical scholars, however, because most view the plurals in this context as a reference to an angelic court surrounding God in heaven. God is thus portrayed here as a king declaring his intentions to the members of his royal council (see 1 Kgs. 2.19–23; Job 1.6–2.6; Ps. 82, 89.7; Isa. 6.1–8; Jer. 23.18).

Another exegetical argument put forward in support of this position focuses on the juxtaposition of the image of God with the declaration that God would create humans to be "male and female" in Genesis 1.27.[20] As Barth famously asked, "Could anything be more obvious than to conclude from this clear indication that the image and likeness of the being created by God signifies existence in confrontation, i.e., in this confrontation, in the juxtaposition and conjunction of man and man which is that of male and female?"[21] As with the functional view, however, we must recognize that the mere juxtaposition of two concepts can only establish a close relationship; it cannot clarify the nature of the relationship. Thus, even though this juxtaposition will press us to consider how human sexuality might be related to the *imago Dei*, we cannot simply assume their direct identity.

A third exegetical arguments looks to the larger context of the creation narratives. As we discussed with respect to the functional approach, this narratival argument contends that Genesis 1 and 2 should be read together and allowed to inform the other's portrayal of human creation. Thus, even if we maintain that there is no direct reference to relationality in the creation account of Genesis 1, the continuation of the creation story in the Genesis narrative moves strongly in that direction. As we move into Genesis 2 we see the human person engaging first in a relationship with God (vv. 8–17), then with creation (vv. 15, 18–20), and finally with other human persons (vv. 21–25). Indeed, although the first creation account presents human persons made in the image of God as "good," the second creation narrative clarifies that this is only true after God creates both male and female human persons and they come together in an interpersonal relationship (vv. 18–25). Moving on to the account of the fall in Genesis 3 contributes to this account as well as the consequences of sin unfold primarily in terms of its impact on human relationships: human–divine (v. 8), human–human (vv. 7, 12, 16), and human–creation (vv. 18–19) relationships. The deterioration of these three relationships continues to be a prominent theme throughout the biblical narratives and suggests that relationality does in fact lie at the core of what it means to be *imago Dei* beings.

These exegetical concerns are often supported by at least two additional theological arguments. First, regardless of whether one sees the divine plural as a reference to the Trinity, most relational theologians argue that the interpersonal nature of the triune God clearly supports the idea that human persons reflect God in their essential relationality. Barth thus relates the divine image to "the differentiation and relationship, the loving co-existence and co-operation, the I and Thou, which first take place in God Himself."[22] Second, many theologians argue that the Christological *imago* of the NT requires such a relational interpretation. If Jesus Christ is the true manifestation of what it means to be made in the image of God, then we must recognize the importance of at least three factors: (1) the fundamental significance of Jesus' relationship with the Father and the Spirit clearly displayed throughout his life (see in particular Jn 1.1–18, 32–33; 5.17–29; 14–16); (2) the emphasis that Jesus placed on interpersonal relationships in his earthly ministry (e.g., the Twelve; Mary, Martha, and Lazarus); and (3) the fact that the result of Jesus' ministry was the constitution of a "new man" comprising human persons brought together in relationship as members of his body (1 Cor. 12.12–31; Eph. 2.15; Col. 3.10).

With respect to the status of the image after the fall, those affirming a more relational approach have tended to argue that the image was completely lost at the fall. Because the fall into sin has separated human persons from God such that they are alienated from him and in need of reconciliation, and because the *imago Dei* is manifest primarily in the human person's relationship with God, it stands to reason that the *imago Dei* ceased once humanity's relationship with God was severed.

However, having said all of this, the relational approach has its own critics. The most common critique is that the relational approach lacks exegetical foundation. Karl Barth's exegesis in particular has come under severe criticism. Thus, James Barr famously derided Barth's exegesis as "particularly ill-judged and irresponsible."[23] At times this criticism goes so far as to claim that the relational approach is entirely without exegetical basis. As we have seen, however, proponents of the relational approach are actually quite concerned to establish an exegetical basis for their understanding. The fact that many biblical scholars find these exegetical arguments unconvincing should not prevent us from recognizing their exegetical endeavors. Indeed, the disagreements often reflect a fundamental difference on the nature of the exegetical task (e.g., the role of the NT in interpreting the OT, the legitimacy of theological interpretation) more than any exegetical ineptitude on the part of relational thinkers.[24]

A related concern is that what exegetical support the relational approach does enjoy is actually driven by an anachronistic tendency to read modern conceptual categories into the biblical text. Phyllis Bird thus criticizes Barth for advancing "an interpretation characterized by the distinctly modern concept of an 'I–Thou' relationship."[25] Given the propensity that theologians have long had for reading their own cultural conceptions of the human into particular formulations of the *imago Dei*, we would be well advised to take the criticism to heart and monitor our own formulations carefully. Nonetheless, any such criticism should be careful not to reject the relational interpretation simply because of the prominence of relationality in modern thought. Although its cultural popularity should give us pause, its adequacy as an interpretation of a biblical text should be weighed on its own merits.

Finally, biblical scholars tend to be deeply suspicious of any attempt to interpret Genesis 1 through a broader theological and canonical framework. For many, the idea that Genesis 1 and 2 were written independently and only later brought together as part of one work means that Genesis 1 should be interpreted without reference to Genesis 2. Regardless of the compositional history of Genesis 1 and 2, however, I have argued that since these two narratives are now located within the same work, we must read them together as part of the same story of creation, albeit told from different perspectives. Biblical scholars are also highly suspicious of attempts to read later theological formulations (e.g., Christ as the image of God) into earlier texts, particularly if that involves reading NT meanings into OT documents. We should certainly be sensitive to this argument and avoid understanding the image of God in Genesis 1–2 in ways that would have been meaningless to the original readers. If the NT authors unveil a new understanding of an OT concept that, while consistent with the OT meaning, transcends it in new and important ways, we certainly need to take that into account.

It would seem, then, that despite criticisms about the exegetically unfounded nature of the relational *imago*, it remains a viable candidate for understanding this important concept.

The multifaceted image

Our last approach to understanding the *imago Dei* has been developed by thinkers who contend that the image of God is a multifaceted concept that cannot be restricted to one set of categories. These scholars argue that the important criticisms leveled against the other three approaches suggest that none of them is sufficient to serve as an adequate explanation of the *imago*. Instead, we should appeal to all three in developing a robust view of the *imago*. As Stanley Grenz argued, the lack of unanimity we have observed regarding the meaning of the *imago Dei* suggests that we should be cautious about viewing it from "too narrow a perspective."[26]

This approach frequently points out that the creation narratives apply the *imago Dei* to the entire human person, not one aspect alone. Thus, God simply declares his intention to create "man" in his image. No hint can be found here that this involves only certain capacities, functions, or relationships; only that the human person as a whole reflects God in creation. Similarly, when *demut* is used to describe the relationship between Seth and Adam (Gen. 5.3), the picture is clearly that of Seth as a whole person reflecting the likeness of his father. Thus, theologians affirming a multifaceted understanding of the *imago* argue that the creation narratives do not focus on one aspect alone but simply declare the whole human person to be *imago Dei*. Consequently, our understanding of what the *imago* is should address all the various aspects of the human person.

Similarly, what is reflected about God in the *imago Dei* is also multifaceted. Rather than focusing on a single facet of the divine nature, these thinkers contend that humans image a variety of different things about God. Echoing Paul in Romans 1.20, this approach portrays the human as imaging in creation many of God's attributes or characteristics.

While affirming the multifaceted nature of the *imago*, some theologians draw a distinction between broader and narrower aspects of the image. For these thinkers, the image of God has a broad, structural sense that refers to any and all of humanity's capacities that have an analogical parallel to the divine being (e.g., capacities for rationality, will, love). In the narrower sense, however, the image of God is properly displayed when these capacities are rightly used to reflect the glory of God. In its fullest sense, however, the image of God is displayed when human persons corporately utilize their God-given capacities in their proper function. Like the patristic distinction between the *image* and *likeness*, this approach typically argues that after the fall the *imago Dei* in its narrower sense was completely lost, but the image in its broader sense remains.

At first glance, this seems like an easy solution to the problem of understanding the image of God. Because the Bible does not give us an explicit definition of the image, and because we have multiple competing proposals for its best explanation, we should just agree with all of them. Nonetheless, a few concerns come to mind.

The most obvious problem would seem to be that of including the structural approach within its framework despite the rather strong objections we raised about that approach earlier—especially its lack of exegetical support and susceptibility to cultural concepts of humanity. Given these concerns, the multifaceted approach is faced with two options. It could offer a defense of the structural *imago* that would address these concerns, or it could drop the structural approach entirely and developed an understanding of the imago that incorporates only the functional and relational approaches. Since the former does not seem very promising, the latter needs to be pursued more clearly.

The multifaceted approach also struggles to explain how the relational and functional concepts might be related to one another. These two ideas are generally understood in a way that makes problematic any attempt to develop them together as a single, coherent theory. It might seem that one could bring the two together by reconstituting relationality as a function, that is, "relating." Any such attempt, however, immediately loses the strength of the functional approach, its exegetical basis. The functional concept of the image of God operative in the ancient near east was not an empty cipher that one can fill with whatever function seems most appropriate. To reconstitute the meaning of the functional *imago* in relational terms would be to justify criticisms that the relational approach anachronistically reads modern categories back into the ancient text. Any multifaceted approach, then, needs to provide an explanation of how it can hold these seemingly disparate theories together while allowing each to retain its own significance.

c. The current state of the debate

As it currently stands, then, the debate over the image of God has led to consensus on a number of important issues, but the fundamental nature of the *imago Dei* in its original intention and in its significance for understanding humanity remains a contested issue. Although the structural approach remains influential at the popular level, it has been rejected by most contemporary thinkers. For some it still serves in a secondary way as an expression either of the capacities necessary for the *imago* or as an expression of creation's common witness to the glory of God, but most have abandoned the structural approach as a core aspect of the *imago Dei*. The functional and relational approaches, on the other hand, retain high levels of support. Indeed, there is a significant divide between biblical scholars and theologians at precisely this point. The general consensus among contemporary biblical scholars is that the image of God in Genesis 1 should be understood in a primarily functional sense; most theologians, on the other hand, argue for a relational approach. To a large degree, this difference is generated by the unresolved hermeneutical question of the proper context within which to understand Genesis 1:26–28. Finally, the multifaceted approach, while enjoying some level of support and growing in popularity, has not yet demonstrated that it is sufficiently coherent to serve as an adequate proposal.

So, the nature of the *imago Dei* remains an important and unresolved issue in contemporary theology. In the next section we will try to find some way of working through these issues and coming to a better understanding of what the *imago Dei* is and how it should inform our understanding of human persons.

A WAY FORWARD: REPRESENTATION, PRESENCE, AND COVENANT IN THE IMAGE OF GOD

The difficulty presented in the contemporary debate is that we find good arguments for and against both the relational and functional approaches to understanding the image of God. We cannot easily set aside the exegetical considerations supporting the functional approach, and we cannot simply dismiss the broader hermeneutical and theological issues raised by proponents of the relational approach. It would seem, then, that our best approach would be to retain both, yet it has not been easy to find a way of negotiating the differences between them. As Nathan MacDonald observes, "Agreement, almost consensus, amongst both sets of scholars cannot disguise the chasm that divides the two. Unfortunately there appears to be little scope for communications across lines firmly drawn."[27]

The task of this section will be to suggest one way of negotiating this tension.

a. The image as representational presence

We can begin by fleshing out the concept of *representation* further. As we discussed earlier, the core concept of the functional imago is that the human person represents God in creation and that this core concept is importantly related to humanity's dominion over creation. What remains to be explained, however, is precisely what it is about the *imago* that warrants the conclusion that representation grounds human rulership. As most acknowledge that the declaration of human dominion ("let them rule") provides a consequence rather than a definition of the image, the functional approach leaves us wondering about the precise nature of the representational function itself

The concept of representation actually involves a range of ideas. For example, let us consider a number of ways that one can represent a country. On a pretty basic level, we can say that a map represents a country, but it does so by merely drawing us a picture of the country's shape. A country's currency, on the other hand, involves the country more directly. I can buy something with a dollar bill, which has no intrinsic value, only because the shop owner understands that the dollar bill actually represents the country's broader financial resources. Unlike a map, a country's currency represents the country in a way that entails the country's participation. This participative function stands out even more clearly when we consider a nation's flag. Although still symbolic, a nation's participation in its flag is so close that it is viewed as actually being "present" where its flag is present. Thus, to defile or disrespect a nation's flag is to defile or disrespect the nation itself. Finally, the representative presence of the country stands out most starkly in the representative function of the nation's ruler. The entire nation is not "actually" present in the person of its ruler. Nonetheless, the presence of the nation in the personal representation of its ruler is at its highest level. From this example, then, we can see that *representation* is a concept that spans a whole range of ideas: from the more abstract and symbolic to the more concrete and personal.

The kind of representation involved in the *imago Dei* functions at the more concrete/relational end of this spectrum. In the ancient near east, a divine image was understood to be far more than a merely symbolic depiction of the divine reality. Instead, an image was identified with a particular manifestation of the divine being's presence and sovereign authority. The image stood in "spiritual union" with the reality it imaged.[28] The physical image of a king (e.g., a statue) was not a mere symbol of the king, but it was actually a manifestation of the king's presence. Similarly, an idol was understood to represent some divine being so closely that the presence of the divine was manifested through it.

If we apply this relationship-as-presence to the *imago Dei*, it becomes clearer how the *imago* grounds the dominical aspect of the image. Because the image actually involves the presence of the one imaged, the image carries with it the authority and dominion of the one imaged as well.

Our concept of the *imago Dei* as it relates to human persons, then, should retain this emphasis on a representation that affirms the presence of the divine reality in the symbol (i.e., the human person) while affirming a real difference between them. Some have argued that this explains the prohibition against creating likenesses of God in the second commandment (Exod. 20.4). Although a different term for likeness is used here (*temunah*), it may well be that the *imago Dei* provides the implicit framework for the command. As God has already created human persons to serve as his image, and consequently as the ones through whom his presence is properly manifest in creation, any attempt to create additional images or likenesses of him is invalid.

Understanding representation as involving the presence of the one represented in a way sufficient to ground the exercise of authority helps the functional approach connect with the Christological reorientation of the idea that takes place in the NT. The NT authors certainly understood the incarnation to involve the real presence of God in and through the humanity of Jesus Christ. Thus, that Christ is "the image of the invisible God" (Col. 1.15) communicates more than that he "reflects" or "makes visible" the invisible qualities of God, although he certainly does that as well. Instead, the emphasis of the NT is on the presence of the divine in the incarnation. Thus, Jesus declares, "The Father is in me, and I in the Father" (Jn 10.38), a thought echoed by Paul in his statement, "In Christ all the fullness of deity lives in bodily form" (Col. 2.9). Thus, Christ is not the true image simply in virtue of the fact that he reflects God's attributes

quantitatively better than the rest of creation, as though even a puri-
fied human nature could ever adequately reflect the qualities and
attributes of an infinite God; rather, Christ is the true image because
he is the true "representative" of God, the one in whom the real
presence of God is manifest in creation.

Once the concept of representation is fleshed out a bit more, then,
we see that the functional *imago* portrays Genesis 1.26–28 as a declaration that human persons are a unique locus of the manifestation
of God's glorious divine presence in creation. It is in virtue of this
representative manifestation of divine presence, consequently, that
humanity exercises dominion in and over creation. In this sense, the
image of God is a *task*, something that the human person performs
in creation. As significant as this is for understanding the image of
God, the relational approach offers a number of important insights
as well.

b. The image as personal presence

In the previous section, we saw that our understanding of the functional approach could be deepened by reflecting more on the nature
of "representation," discovering that the *imago* is best understood
through the motif of representational presence. The relational
approach to the image will cause us to reflect on this notion a little
more by pressing us to think about what we mean by "presence."
In the creation accounts, and throughout the rest of the biblical
narratives, God's manifests his presence as a *personal* presence.

The manifestation of God's presence as a personal presence is seen
immediately in the creation accounts as God encounters humanity
by engaging, even constituting, them as personal beings.[29] In both
creation accounts, God initiates the Creator/creature relationship and
brings humanity into existence. Yet the narratives are clear that this
relationships is not simply the cause and effect of the Creator/creature
relationship but is, in fact, a relationship in which there is personal
engagement and dialog. Each narrative marks the human out as the
creature to whom God speaks, expresses his desire, and expects a
response. God thus initiates the kind of relationship that we associate with persons—a relationship that involves "an encounter between
two or more partners who are different, who have some independence
and autonomy in the relation and who may therefore engage with
each other on the basis of freedom rather than coercion."[30] God

manifests himself to humanity as a personal being by creating and constituting humans as personal beings.

The significance of the personal for humanity unfolds even more clearly in the second narrative. Although the human is created in personal relationship to God at the beginning of the story, God still looks at the individual human person and declares that "it is not good for him to be alone" (Gen. 2.18). This stands in marked contrast to the earlier "it was very good" (Gen. 1.31) and comes as a bit of a surprise because Adam was not in fact "alone"; indeed, he was already engaged in a personal relationship with God himself. Nonetheless, God declares the divine/human relationship to be lacking something necessary for humanity.

Likewise, the relationship of humans to other creatures cannot provide everything that the human needs. In 2.19–20 the human is brought into relation with all of the other created animals, but none of them was deemed appropriate for Adam. The text does not indicate the nature of the lack, however, stating only that no other creature was a "suitable helper" for Adam. In the OT, *ezer* ("helper") refers primarily to someone (often God) who protects and/or aids another in some way.[31] The specific nature of the assistance depends on the context of the term's use (e.g., providing military assistance, helping the poor). Although the text is not explicit, Adam's need for an *ezer* suggests that Adam faces a task that cannot be accomplished alone and that other creatures are not suitable to help him accomplish. The nature of the task and the assistance required, await further clarification.

The narrative thus far has established the solitary human person needs an *ezer* to satisfy his being and that this is not a role that can be filled by God or by other creatures. We thus move on to the third relationship, that between the male and female. Faced with the lack of a suitable *ezer* that would enable Adam to perform his task, Adam is confronted with one who is fully human (vv. 21–23), of the same nature as Adam (i.e., "flesh of my flesh") but who is still different from him. As with the divine/human relationship, this too is constituted by address and response. Although the woman does not speak in the narrative, the meeting of man and woman, the man's response to her, and the depiction of relationship and intimacy in the concluding verse, all clearly support that this is a personal relationship. Here again we see "the call and response, the gift and return of dialogue" that characterizes personal relations.[32] It would seem, then, that what the solitary human individual could not accomplish was the coming together in personal relationship of beings who are both distinct from one another and yet of the same nature as the other. For this, Adam required an *ezer*, and his *ezer* could not be found in God, who is not of the same nature as Adam or other creatures, who were not constituted as personal beings. The climax of the creation account, then, is not the bare fact of humanity's creation, or humanity's status as rulers/caretakers of creation. Instead, the narrative culminates with the advent of human personal relationship, with the coming together of the two who are same yet different in personal relationship (2.24–25).

Having argued that personal relationship lies at the heart of the creation narratives, we are still left wondering why human-to-human personal relationship is so vital for understanding the *imago Dei*. If it were merely the personal relationship that was the issue, would not the divine/human relationship have sufficed? I argued above that the functional interpretation was best understood as *representational presence*. As we have seen in the creation narratives, however, God's presence with human persons is a personal presence that constitutes personal relationships. The image of God, then, is best understood not simply as a manifestation of God's presence but as a manifestation of his *personal* presence. Consequently, the problem of the individual human derives from the fact that the individual human is incapable of manifesting God's presence, his *personal* presence, in creation. The creation of humanity as male and female, then, serves to constitute the interpersonal relationality in which God has chosen to manifest himself.[33]

c. The image as covenantal presence

Thus far, I have argued that the *imago Dei* should be understood as something that the human person does, a task that the human persons perform. It would actually be more proper to say that the *imago Dei* is something that God does (i.e., manifests himself) in and through human persons, a task in which human persons are called to participate. In this sense, the *imago Dei* is a gift given to humanity by God through the divine summons and the creation of human persons as male and female so that they might manifest his personal presence in creation. In this way, the functional and relational come together as a task that is already a gift. As important as both of these elements are, however, we still need to add one further item to our understanding of the image of God—the *imago Dei* as covenantal narrative.

As Karl Barth quite rightly pointed out, Genesis 1 is the "prologue" to a much larger narrative.[34] Human persons are introduced in this prologue as the divine image bearers with the hint that the nature of this image bearing is to manifest God's presence in creation. In the following chapter the *imago Dei* unfolds through God's covenantal relationship with humanity and through humanity's interpersonal relationality with one another. This story continues with the devastating impact of sin on human persons and creation as a whole. Although sin shatters the *shalom* of creation, God continues to manifest his personal presence in and through his relationship with human persons and their relationship with one another as witnessed in the history of his relationships with Israel and the Church.[35] Thus, although we can say in one sense that God continues to manifest his presence through all human persons as his image bearers, there is another and vitally important sense in which God's presence is most clearly evidenced in his covenantal relationship with his people. It is in the context of this covenantal relationship that God manifests himself as the "I am" who continues his covenantal relationship with humanity despite their rejection of him. Rather than something "possessed" by human persons as a part of their essential being, then, the image of God is shown to be something that unfolds over time as God manifests himself in and through the narrative of his covenantal relationship with humanity. As Michael Horton argues,

> We will therefore look for an answer to the question, "What is it to be human?" not in ontological definitions of inner states or essences, much less in terms of contrasts with the nonhuman creation, but in terms of the unique *commission* given to human beings in the biblical narrative. For the biblical writers at least, "What is it to be human?" is ultimately a narrative-ethical rather than a metaphysical-ontological question.[36]

This narrative climaxes with the coming of the one who truly manifests the personal presence of God, Jesus Christ, and the initiation of a community of image bearers who are being transformed and renewed into the likeness of the Messiah. This narrative, of course, remains incomplete as we await its eschatological culmination. Thus, as Stanley Grenz has argued, our understanding of the *imago Dei* must be forged from this "entire salvation-historical narrative, climaxing in the new humanity and the eschatological community."[37] The human person as a divine image bearer has a narratival history and, consequently, "a temporal direction,"[38] the entirety of which must be brought to bear on our understanding of what it means to serves as God's representatives through whom God's personal presence is manifest in creation.

The image of God, then, is best understood when we bring together all three of these elements. First, the image of God is the task in which human persons serve as God's representatives by manifesting his presence in creation. Second, the image of God involves God creating and constituting humans as personal beings through whom he can manifest himself personally in creation. Third, the image of God involves the continual unfolding of God's personal being as he manifests himself in and through his covenantal relationships with his people, Israel and the Church. Putting these three elements together, then, the image of God can be understood as *God manifesting his personal presence in creation through his covenantal relationships with human persons, whom he has constituted as personal beings to serve as his representatives in creation and to whom he remains faithful despite their sinful rejection of him.*

CONCLUSION

Despite a long history of understanding the *imago Dei* as referring to an attribute, capacity, or structure of the human person, we have seen that there are good reasons for understanding it instead as a function, whereby God manifests his personal, covenantal presence in and through human persons. Thus, the affirmation that human persons are created in the image of God should not be understood primarily as an attempt to define what it means to be human. Rather, the *imago Dei* serves to place human persons in a particular theological and narratival context. As such, the *imago Dei* stands at the center of any adequate theological anthropology and will have important consequences for how we approach other anthropological issues. It may be helpful, then, to summarize some of the key anthropological implications of this approach to the *imago* before we move on to the next chapters.

1. *Jesus Christ is the revelation of true humanity.* The starting point of any anthropology informed by the *imago Dei* must, of course, be the centrality of the person and work of Jesus Christ. Even though a robust anthropology will certainly view the human person from a variety of angles, using a number of number conceptual tools, the fundamental perspective of a Christian anthropology must always be the reality manifest in him. Although many have affirmed the centrality of Christ for Christian living—that is, the *imitatio Christi*—a consistently Christocentric anthropology should press beyond this and consider as well the ways in which Christology should inform our understanding of the entire human person.[39]

2. *Human persons are part of and yet unique within creation.* Although I have argued that we should reject the structural understanding of the *imago*, it nonetheless provided us with a good opportunity to reflect on the fact that human persons are fundamentally a part of creation. Although we should not downplay the ways in which human persons are also unique within creation, we must avoid the temptation to overemphasize our uniqueness. Human persons are created beings and share most, if not all, of their creaturely capacities with other animals. Indeed, the biblical narratives make no attempt to single out structural capacities that are unique to the human person, a silence that modern science confirms. We do not need to downplay this to affirm the uniqueness and dignity of the human person as well. However, if Jesus Christ is the revelation of true humanity, we do not learn about what it is to be human at the most fundamental level through a comparison with other animals. It is certainly helpful to do this and we should not deny the valuable contributions that have been made through such studies, but this creaturely perspective will always be limited in establishing what it means to be truly and fully human.

3. *Human persons are mysterious beings.* There are depths to humanity that will always escape our attempts to understand and define the human essence. This is so for at least three reasons. First, because human persons image an infinite, transcendent, and mysterious God, there will always be something at the core of the human person that evades our grasp. Second, to the extent that

the image of God involves the narrative of God's covenantal relationality with humanity, a narrative that is yet incomplete, the nature of the human person will remain hidden in the yet-to-be ending of that story. Third, there seems to be something about personal beings and personal relationship that requires such resistance to epistemological closure. As many thinkers have pointed out, being personal and being involved in personal relationships involves some level of freedom. If the "other" could be secured and fully understood, the "other" would cease to be personal but would instead be an object of possession. For all of these reasons, although the *imago Dei* must serve as an essential starting point for theological anthropology, it will in no way provide an explanation of the human person that finally solves the "riddle" of humanity.[40]

4. *Human persons are relational beings.* As we have seen, human persons are always already involved in several key relationships. Human persons are called into personal being through the divine address and express that personal being through relationships with other human persons and other creatures. Thus, the human person is surrounded and in many ways constituted by these various relationships. This fundamental relationality is witnessed as well in the creation of the "new man" in Christ as an ecclesial community. An adequate theological anthropology, then, must understand the human person as an ecclesial being constituted in and for relationship.[41]

5. *Human persons are responsible beings.* In the divine address, human persons are constituted as personal beings and, consequently, as beings with the opportunity and responsibility to respond. Our anthropology, then, must account for this basic responsibility. As personal relationship cannot exist without some level of freedom to relate, this entails that we see the human person as having whatever kind of freedom is necessary to support personal relationship and responsibility. We must also recognize that the divine address that personalizes the human being is not a mere word of greeting but a summons that makes a moral demand. The capacity and opportunity to respond to the divine address entails, therefore, that the human person is a morally responsible being. Human persons are capable of making (or not making) morally significant decisions for which they can and will be held responsible.

6. *Human persons are embodied beings*. We must also affirm that the creation of human beings as *imago Dei* emphasizes that humans are embodied beings. As we have seen, the *imago Dei* is not something applied to the "inner," "immaterial," or "spiritual" dimensions of the human person. On the contrary, the *imago* encompasses the embodied human person as a whole. I image God as a physical being with all of its related capacities, incapacities, and needs.[42] Indeed, it would seem that it is only as embodied beings that we can function as God's representatives in a physical world, and many will argue that it is only as embodied beings that humans can stand in vital relationships with one another. Any anthropology that neglects the embodied reality of human life, then, must be rejected.

7. *Human persons are broken*. Finally, our consideration of the *imago Dei* has also led us to recognize that humanity as we now know it is broken. Everything about human persons and human existence since the fall stands under the pervasive influence of sin. Any adequate anthropology must address the fact that real humanity as we actually see and experience it is corrupted by sin. Consequently, we cannot arrive at an understanding of true humanity— humanity as God intended it to be and which God is restoring in and through the person of Jesus Christ—through empirical observations of humanity as it actually is. Once again, then, we are led back to the person and work of Jesus Christ, the righteous one, as the only adequate starting point for a valid theological anthropology.

Together, affirmations must serve as the building blocks for our understanding of the human person. As we work through the rest of these chapters, we will continually return to the core truth that human persons are *imago Dei* beings. Any attempt to answer questions about human sexuality, volitionality, or ontology, among other things, begins here.

CHAPTER 3

SEXUALITY

Thus sex remains a profound and baffling enigma of personal existence, the mystery of which can never be dispelled by excogitation—and certainly not by studying what is now both popularly and scientifically called "sex."

D. S. Bailey[1]

Children have a remarkable aptitude for pointing out those areas in which we do not know as much as we think we do. "Daddy, what is a 'boy'?" How exactly should I respond to my four-year old daughter? Had she asked me more generically whether I knew what the term "boy" meant, I would have confidently asserted that I did. This question, however, asks for a specific definition of "boy" and reveals more ambiguity in my understanding than I might have realized at first. What does it mean to be "boy"? Should I offer a biological answer to the question (ignoring the fact that she's only four and would have a hard time understanding what chromosomes and hormones have to do with being a boy)? Maybe it would be better to go with a more behavioral answer, focusing on the stereotypical behaviors we often use to distinguish boys from girls (which, according to my daughter, mostly involves the boys getting into trouble a lot). Or, maybe I should just stick with the purely superficial issues of appearance (dress, hair style, etc.) that my daughter seems most concerned about. (She was particularly concerned that getting her hair cut would turn her into a boy.) Each of these demonstrates that my earlier confidence in my ability to define "boy" was rather naïve. As we move through this chapter and reflect more deeply on what terms like "male," "female," "gender," and "sexuality" mean when applied to human persons, we will come to realize that these are complex terms that involve more than their face value might suggest. We think we know what they mean until someone asks us to define them. The more that we reflect upon them, the more we realize that the mystery of the human person lurks behind such terms in ways that we can only strive to understand.

That human sexuality is an important issue for understanding humanity should come as no great surprise. Indeed, in many ways, sexuality is an unavoidable anthropological reality. Humans are born as "sexed" beings and spend much of their lives understanding precisely what this means. As Robert Jewett affirms,

> Sexuality permeates one's individual being to its very depth; it conditions every facet of one's life as a person. As the self is always aware of itself as an "I," so this "I" is always aware of itself as himself or herself. Our self-knowledge is indissolubly bound up not simply with our human being but with our sexual being. At the human level there is no "I and thou" per se, but only the "I" who is male or female confronting the "thou," the "other," who is also male and female.[2]

Who we are as human persons, then, is intimately connected to and inseparable from who we are as sexual beings. Consequently, understanding what it means to be a "sexual" being is an unavoidable task for theological anthropology.

At the same time, human sexuality stands at the core of some of today's most heated debates in society and the church. Indeed, "few contemporary issues generate as much heat and conflict in society, and within the church, as those having to do with human sexuality."[3] Debates about homosexuality, marriage, male/female differences, the roles of men and women in church leadership, and many other issues related to sexual morality, identity, and behavior, all swirl around human sexuality.

At the core of each of these debates stand certain ideas about what it means to be human, what it means to be a sexual being, and how we should live our lives as sexual human beings in community with one another. Each of these issues has strong proponents on every side contending that theirs is the most adequate way of understanding how human sexuality should function in society. Unfortunately, however, these debates seldom address a more fundamental set of questions. What is human sexuality? How does sexuality inform and affect what it means to be human? Furthermore, what is the theological significance of human sexuality? Instead, people on all sides of each debate tend to assume that "male" and "female" are known realities. For such thinkers, the challenging question is how we understand the relationship between male and female in society and the church. But, how can we make any progress in understanding the proper relation and function of human sexuality without first wrestling with what sexuality is and how it is related to being human? Lacking an answer to this question, we address issues of sexual morality and behavior on the basis of implicit, pre-reflective ideas about the nature of human sexuality, ideas that guide and influence our conclusions and positions without themselves becoming the objects of critical consideration. Our task in this chapter, then, will be to raise some of the issues and questions that need to be addressed if we are going to begin developing an explicit and theologically informed understanding of what it means to affirm that human persons are sexual beings.[4]

WHAT IS "GENDER"?

I imagine that when I was born, the doctor declared to my parents, "It's a boy!" But what exactly has the doctor done in declaring me to be a "boy"? What kind of a statement is this? From one perspective, the doctor has made a purely scientific observation about the nature of my sexual anatomy. Having the external genitalia of a male human, the doctor observes that I am, in fact, a boy. However, if this is all that the doctor is doing, why is it that sexuality is always the first thing that doctors comment on? Surely, the sexual genitalia are not the most notable features of a newborn child. The doctor could have made equally objective observations about the size of my head or the tone of my skin. The doctor notes my sexuality, however, because she is doing more than simply making an objective assessment of a newborn body. At the same time, she is also performing a cultural act. She has named me as "boy," not just a human but one who belongs to a particular category of human and who will now receive the treatment, expectations, and benefits/detriments typically associated with those in that group.

As we reflect, then, on what the doctor has done in declaring my gender, we run into a number of important questions. To what extent is human sexuality determined by purely biological considerations? What role does society and culture play in forming the meaning of terms such as "boy" and "girl"? How significant is gender for understanding what it means to be human? All of these questions must be engaged to some extent in our pursuit of a theological understanding of gender. As we move through this chapter, we will begin to understand that human sexuality is a complex reality that can only be understood once a variety of factors are accounted for. Most important, we will see that human sexuality is constituted partly by biological factors and partly by cultural factors, but that it is ultimately grounded in theological factors. The first two of those issues, the biological and cultural, will be the focus of this section.

a. Androgyny and "ideal" humanity

Humans are sexual creatures. While we might not understand exactly what that means, there seems little doubt that humanity as we experience it is sexed. Indeed, in our modern culture, it is difficult to go anywhere without being confronted by the sexuality of the human race. It might come as a bit of a surprise, then, to discover that many have argued that sexuality is not a fundamental aspect of human nature. Instead, they contend that sexuality is, at best, a superficial characteristic of a more fundamental humanity that is shared by all human persons. I am first and foremost, from this perspective, a human being. The fact that I am also "male" is, at best, a secondary characteristic that shapes human identity, or, at worst, a consequence of sin from which I hope to escape someday. Either way, sexuality is not fundamental to human nature.

According to one of the oldest ways of understanding humanity, there is an essential human nature that underlies gender and gender differences—a true "asexual" humanity that is more fundamental than "male" or "female" humanity. Understanding true humanity, then, requires that we look beyond the sexual polarity of humanity as we now see it and seek out the unity of our common humanity. Indeed, for many thinkers in this tradition, our sexual polarity is not just a secondary and more superficial characteristic, but it is actually a result of sin and should not factor into our understanding of true humanity in any way.

Some see support for this basic androgyny in the creation narratives. On this reading, God originally created true humanity as the genderless "adam" (Gen. 2.7)[5] and only subsequently separates the "adam" into male and female (Gen. 2.21–22).[6] This sexual bifurcation, however, is not a merely neutral act but is actually a "consequence" of sin.[7] Although temporally prior to the fall, God created sexuality in anticipation of humanity's fall and the need to provide a mechanism for human reproduction in its fallen state.[8] Others look to Jesus' description of the resurrection as support for their position, "At the resurrection people will neither marry nor be given in marriage; they will be like the angels in heaven" (Mt. 22.30). The argument here seems to run along two trajectories. First, the assumption is often made that because (1) there is no marriage in heaven, (2) marriage is primarily about sexual reproduction, and (3) sexual reproduction requires sexual diversification, (4) there will be no gender diversification in heaven. In heaven, we will return to the androgynous ideal of our original state. The second argument has to do with the reference to the angels. Because angels are asexual beings, the fact that Jesus says we will be like the angels means that we too will be asexual in our eschatological state.

This way of construing human nature, however, is fundamentally flawed for a number of reasons. First, the appeal to androgyny in the biblical texts is unconvincing at best. The creation narratives simply do not indicate that human sexuality is a result of the fall. Indeed, the narratives explicitly indicate otherwise. It is difficult to escape the conclusion that the only reason for reading the creation narratives in this way is a prior determination that human sexuality is a necessary evil. The argument from Jesus' statement about the resurrection is similarly unconvincing. Jesus statement about the resurrection is not about gender and sexuality but about marriage. His point is rather simple: you do not need to worry about who you will be married to in heaven because human relationships will not be based on marriage in heaven. A little later, we will see that there are good theological reasons for this temporal limitation on marriage. A second, and related, point is that the comparison with angels does not refer to the ostensibly asexual nature of the angels. Instead, Jesus' point is that the angels do not marry and neither will we. Third, the argument assumes that the exclusive function of gender is to facilitate sexual reproduction. If human sexuality has a broader purpose than reproduction alone, however, then it is entirely possible that it might continue in the eschatological state even if sexual reproduction is not a part of the eschaton.

In addition to these exegetical problems, androgyny should be criticized to the extent that it posits an abstract human nature, a substratum of humanness that underlies our merely superficial sexuality. Regardless of what one thinks about abstract natures, this approach neglects the fact that humanity as we have it is always already gendered. There are no abstract, androgynous humans—only sexual ones.

This concern leads to another. By emphasizing an abstract human nature, this approach can only lead to an implicit neglect of human embodiment. To the extent that we emphasize an androgynous ideal, we necessarily marginalize embodiment and its significance for understanding human persons. Yet marginalizing sexuality is something that we simply cannot do. Most psychologists recognize that sexuality is fundamental for understanding humanity and human identity, something demonstrated by the fact that all cultures make some distinction between the sexes.[9] In addition, a theology that is informed by the incarnation and the resurrection cannot afford to neglect the importance of human embodiment. Jesus did not come to us as the incarnation of an abstract human nature; he came as a sexual human being. Although we have little information about the particulars of Jesus' resurrection body, or our own, we also have no reason to think that our resurrection bodies will not be gendered. There is no indication that Jesus was no longer a male human after his resurrection, something that certainly would have warranted some comment in the narratives. Thus, if our theological anthropology "is rooted in reflection on the person of Jesus Christ," there is no room for denigration of the human body.[10]

Finally, we should recognize that despite the affirmation of an androgynous ideal that is neither male nor female, androgyny has historically taken some concept of the "male" as normative for true humanity. Thus, rather than presenting a genderless ideal, the androgynous approach often expresses the characteristics associated with the ideal male in a given society. Thus, as Simone de Beauvoir commented, "Man is defined as a human being and a woman as a female—whenever she behaves as a human being she is said to imitate the male."[11] This approach has gone so far as to view the female as a faulty expression of the true, male ideal.[12] More often, this sublimation of the female is unintentional but the effect remains very real.

Drawing on these arguments, theologians conclude that sexuality "goes down to the very roots of our personal existence"[13] penetrating "to the core of human existence and personhood."[14] Sexuality cannot be set aside as a superficial characteristic of a more fundamental human nature but is itself a basic aspect of human existence. Unless significantly reformulated, androgyny fails to satisfy any anthropology that seeks to take seriously the reality of human embodiment—as informed by the doctrines of creation, incarnation, and resurrection—and the fundamental significance of human sexuality.

b. Biology and the "essential" nature of gender

A more common way of understanding human sexuality is to see it as something that is a biological "given." Being male or female results from the genetic coding with which a person is born. Researchers have identified at least six different biological factors that have a bearing on one's sexuality[15]:

- *chromosomal sex:* the chromosomes that are determined by one's genetic constitution;
- *gonadal sex*: whether a person develops either testes or ovaries *in utero*;
- *fetal hormonal sex*: the relative amounts of estrogen and testosterone produced *in utero*;
- *internal organ sex*: the kinds of internal and external organs that the fetus develops;
- *pubertal hormonal sex:* the relative amounts of testosterone and estrogen produced by the person at puberty.

Each stage of development, and the corresponding biological influences, produces a different result in the developing human person, leading to significant differences between men and women—for example, size, body shape, and sexual organs. Beyond these basic biological considerations, a number of recent studies have also argued that biology plays a prominent role in the development of psychological traits associated with gender development. Several have demonstrated the significance of hormonal levels at key points in the development of psychological attributes, personality differences, behavior, and even occupational choices.[16] Many thus conclude that "infants enter the world with some predispositions to 'masculinity' and 'femininity,' and these predispositions appear to result largely from hormones to which they were exposed before birth."[17]

This approach has two basic consequences. First, gender comes to be understood as an essential aspect of human nature, and is, therefore, necessary for understanding true humanity. Human persons are always sexual beings, so there is no more fundamental, asexual human nature that we need to seek in our pursuit to understand humanity. Second, because gender bifurcation is a natural and necessary feature of the human world, the gender differences that arise as a result of this sexual differentiation (or, at least, most of them) are also natural features of the world. Men are generally bigger, stronger, and more aggressive than women, and this stems naturally from humanity's biological essence.

Gender essentialists marshal a number of important arguments in favor of their position. Most significantly, they typically cite a slew of studies that support the idea that there are fundamental differences between men and women: biological, psychological, emotional, social, and so forth.[18] Not only do these studies suggest that there are consistent differences between men and women but that at least some of these differences transcend temporal and cultural differences.[19] To the extent that this is true, gender essentialists argue that we can be confident that human sexuality and the corresponding differences are natural and essential aspects of being human.

In addition to the scientific data, gender essentialists often appeal to the Bible in support of their position. Because God created humans as male and female, they argue, gender must be an essential and natural part of human nature. The intrinsic differences that exist between men and women, then, are also expressions of God's creational purposes and any attempt to "blur the lines" between male and female should be viewed as an irresponsible attempt to do away with divinely ordained distinctions.[20]

Gender essentialism has its problems, however. Most important, as we will see in the next section, cultural and environmental influences plays a much stronger role in determining gender differences and how we interpret them than essentialists typically acknowledge. Although we must account for the scientific and theological arguments in favor of essentialism and these will press us to acknowledge ways in which at least some differences are essentially rooted in biology, we will see in the next section that much of what we think of as gender is less natural and essential than the essentialists would have us believe.

As with the androgynous approach, we must also question whether gender essentialism has really led to us true humanity or whether it has allowed its understanding of essential maleness and femaleness to be determined by its own cultural location. Indeed, studies of the "essential" male and the "essential" female in various contexts indicate that these concepts are strongly influenced by cultural conceptions of male and female. Is it not possible, indeed even likely, that the very studies utilized by gender essentialists to support their conclusions are themselves influenced by their culture's understanding of sexuality? The very questions that such studies ask and the issues they explore are often driven by underlying cultural presuppositions that necessarily color their outcomes. Of course, the interpretation of that data is also open to the shaping influence of these cultural concepts. So, we must be on guard against the possibility that what such research has found to be the "natural" expression of true human sexuality is in fact a projection of a particular cultural ideal.

We must also question their conclusion that humanity's creation as male and female supports gender essentialism; or, at least, we must question whether it supports the kind of gender essentialism they usually have in mind. We certainly should affirm that according to the biblical narratives, God created human persons as sexualized beings. Human sexuality, then, is a natural and essential aspect of humanity. This does not mean, however, that any particular expression of, or interpretation of, human sexuality must be viewed as natural and essential. We must be ever mindful of our sinful proclivity for idealizing our preferences and experiences as expressions of something necessary and essential about humanity. As we discussed in the previous chapter, the current sinful state of humanity should caution us about moving too quickly from the "is" discovered by empirical research to the "ought" of human nature and existence.

c. Culture and the "shaping" of gender

By the latter part of the twentieth century the essentialist approach to understanding gender was coming under increasing criticism as researchers began to appreciate the role that socio-cultural context plays in the development of gender. "A consensus was emerging that gender does not comprise core traits of the individual but rather it is a social construction manufactured and sustained by stereotypical beliefs and social settings. . . . Stated simply, gender is something that is done to us by society, not something we are born with."[21] As Simone de Beauvoir famously declared, "One is not born, but rather becomes, a woman."[22]

Operating from this perspective, many began making a distinction between "sex"—one's biological sex as determined by things such as chromosomes, internal and external genitalia, and so on—and "gender"—the social performance of cultural expectations associated with each sex.[23] One's sex came to be viewed as the biological foundation upon which a particular cultural understanding of gender was constructed—biology provides the "what" of sexuality and culture provides the "how." This approach has been labeled "the coat-rack view" of gender because it portrays our sexed bodies as "the site upon which gender is constructed."[24] "According to this interpretation, all humans are either male or female; their sex is fixed. But cultures interpret sexed bodies differently and project different norms on those bodies thereby creating feminine and masculine persons."[25] We can call this the *weak-constructivist* approach to sexuality as it seeks to affirm the truths of essentialism while recognizing the importance of cultural factors in gender development.

Other researches, however, are dissatisfied with this partial approach. These *strong-constructivists* contend that the biological and cultural aspects of one's sexuality cannot be so neatly bifurcated and that there is no biological "foundation" for sexuality that lies beyond the reach of linguistic and cultural influences. "They do not regard sex, biology, and bodies as prediscursive 'givens' . . . . What are taken as biological facts are actually situated understandings lodged within webs of assumptions that shift from one cultural setting to another, from one epoch to another, and perhaps from one subgroup to another within the same culture."[26] Consequently, they question whether we can even talk about an "objectively" given biological sex.

On the surface, the claim that biological sex is entirely socially constructed seems absurd. Even if we affirm that certain aspects of what it means for me to be "male" in my society are socially determined, isn't it simply obvious that I am *biologically* male? Certainly this must be an objectively given reality. If we probe the question a little further, however, we will see that the "givenness" of biological sex is not as obvious as it might first appear. For one thing, we should realize that even those aspects of gender that seem most clearly driven by biological considerations are more socially and environmentally influenced than we realize. For example, a number of studies have argued that the differences in size of the *corpus callosum* in men and women account for several behavioral and psychological differences.[27] To many, this is a clear example of a gender difference that is rooted in biology. However, even if such differences exist, it remains to be established that this difference is entirely biological. The structures of the brain are highly sensitive to environmental inputs. Our brains are malleable; they are actually shaped by our experiences. So, even if the *corpus callosum* differs in men and women, it remains entirely possible that the differences result from different environmental stimuli—particularly differential treatment stemming from gender stereotypes.[28] This possibility becomes even more likely when we consider that these differences have been found exclusively in adult brains; similar differences have not yet been established in infants. This would suggest that such differences develop in response to environmental stimuli. So, what looked at first like a straightforward biological difference is actually open to cultural construction in important ways. Similar possibilities arise when we consider studies on hormone levels and corresponding behavioral and psychological differences. Environmental factors can act in many ways to "accentuate or act to mitigate the differences induced by hormones."[29] Thus, even those arguing that hormones play a prominent role in the development of gender characteristics, acknowledge that they are not solely determinative and that we need to be aware of nonbiological influences.[30]

Strong constructivists will often argue that the very bifurcation of sexuality into two genders is itself a cultural construct. Consider the famous case of Olympic athlete Maria Patiño. For many years, it was a common practice to test female athletes to verify that they were in fact women. In 1985, Maria Patiño underwent this testing. Although she had female genitalia and had always understood herself to be female—as had her family, friends, and fiancée—she was surprised to discover that she was, in fact, a male. Or, at least, it was discovered that she had XY chromosomes instead of the female-typical XX chromosomes. Because that was the standard used by the athletic commission to determine one's sex, she was determined to be a male and excluded from competition. This condition, known as complete androgen insensitivity, prevents a person's body from processing testosterone. Thus, although her body produced testosterone like a typical male, her body could not process it. As a result, her body developed in more female-typical ways.[31] People with this condition are not alone in their gender ambiguity. Other conditions such as congenital adrenal hyperplasia and reductase deficiency lead to similar gender ambiguity.[32] Thus, although it is certainly the case that most cultures think about gender in binary, male–female terms,[33] some cultures acknowledge a subgroup that does not fit neatly into this schema.[34] Strong constructivists conclude form this that we should be careful about a simplistic reification of our binary gender schemas.[35]

From data such as this, strong constructivists argue that our bodies are not the "given" in this equation. Instead, "our sexed bodies are themselves discursively constructed: they are the way they are, at least to a substantial extent, because of what is attributed to sexed bodies and how they are classified."[36] Gender is not an essential, biological reality given at birth; instead it is a role (or a set of roles) that one learns to "perform" in a particular social setting. Rather than "being" a particular gender, we should talk about "doing gender" in particular ways.[37] This does not mean that gender differences are completely unrelated to biological differences. Given the many studies that strongly support the biological roots of gender, such a position would clearly be untenable. Rather, the constructivists want us to realize that neither sex nor gender is created in a biological vacuum. Instead, biology and culture work together both to shape our bodies and to mold our experiences and their interpretations. Thus, biology does influence gender, but it does so as something that is always–already shaped by culture.

Nonetheless, we can question whether a thoroughgoing constructivism can provide an adequate basis from which to understand human sexuality. Although a carefully nuanced constructivist position might acknowledge the importance of both biology and culture in the shaping one's sexuality, the rhetoric of strong constructivism often suggests otherwise. Thus, for Judith Butler, the idea that sexuality has any essential biological foundation is merely illusory.[38] Sex and gender are both social constructions all the way down. Such an approach, however, cannot but fail to appreciate the valid insights of the essentialist perspective.

We should also note that there is at least one important flaw in the way that the constructivist argument is typically presented.

It presumes that because biology can be culturally/environmentally *influenced,* then biology must be culturally/environmentally *determined.* Such a conclusion, however, is simply unwarranted. It remains entirely possible that at least some fundamental differences are grounded in biological realities, which then influence and are influenced by socio-cultural factors. In other words, if the relationship between biology and culture in the production of gender is best understood as a spiral in which each continually influences the other, it remains entirely possible that the spiral begins with biological considerations.

A third critique can be raised about the constructivist understanding of what it means to be human. Unlike androgyny, which viewed sexuality as a secondary addition to a more fundamental humanity, constructivism contends that there is no fundamental humanity. Human persons are socially constructed all the way through; even the most "objective" aspect of ourselves, our bodies, are social events. There is no "truth" of what it means to be human; there are only culturally particular performances of humanity. As we discussed in the previous chapter, however, the fact that humans are made in the image of God points to a truth about human persons in relationship to God that goes beyond human social construction.[39]

d. Toward an understanding of gender

Each of these different approaches to gender provides a helpful perspective on human sexuality. Androgyny serves to direct our attention to that which men and women have in common, rather than continuously emphasizing the ways in which they differ. That men and women differ is virtually undisputed today.[40] It is all too easy, however, to overstate the significance of these differences. People talk easily about men and women as "opposite sexes," having such fundamental differences that we can view them as coming from different planets.[41] Yet, as many researchers have pointed out, the similarities between men and women vastly outweigh the differences. As Dorothy Sayers aptly argued,

> The first thing that strikes the careless observer is that women are unlike men. They are the "opposite sex"—(though why "opposite" I do not know; what is the "neighbouring sex"?). But the fundamental thing is that women are more like men than

anything else in the world. They are human beings. Vir is male and Femina is female: but Homo is male and female.[42]

Indeed, even those statistical differences that do exist typically show more variability *within* the genders than *between* them.[43] Rather than talk about "opposite sexes," then, most researchers now prefer to think of gender differences and similarities as existing on a continuum, where various individuals may incline toward one polarity or the other, rather than as "a dichotomous arrangement whereby the groups are either similar or different."[44] For example, we typically think of things like dominance and aggressiveness as specifically male characteristics. And, indeed, there is some evidence to suggest that male-typical levels of testosterone contribute to aggressive behavior.[45] Nonetheless, would anyone really want to argue that women cannot be aggressive or act dominantly? Of course not. Many women behave in just this way. When they do so, however, we often say that they are acting "like a man." Why is that? Even if the characteristic occurs more frequently in men than in women, why treat it as an exclusively masculine characteristic if we have just agreed that it is often a characteristic of female behavior as well? Why not say that it is a human characteristic that is embodied in varying degrees by different people? Similar questions could be raised about so-called feminine characteristics like being compassionate or nurturing. Thus, many conclude that we should be very careful about assigning specific characteristics to particular genders. Instead, they contend that it would be better to speak of "gender associated asymmetries," than gender "differences,"[46] and to focus on fostering the development of positive attributes in all human persons regardless of the gender with which we normally associate those attributes.

To this extent, androgyny offers a helpful corrective to the essentialist position and its tendency to overemphasize the differences between the genders. We need to be careful with this androgynous insight, however, if it begins to move in the direction of an amorphous, asexual human nature that denies the possibility of any essential differences. A better approach would strive to retain the insights of each perspective: men and women are importantly different, but exclusively identifying particular characteristics with one gender or the other may be unnecessary and unwise. Thus, James Nelson appeals to the image of a duet in which two distinct instruments come together to play a single tune:

> The image of the duet is significant, for while the harmonious blend is present there are still two instruments playing. Yet, when genuine artistry is present, one is less aware of the separateness and individuality of violinist and pianist than of the beautiful interplay between them. Likewise, the so-called masculine and feminine traits are not dissolved into undifferentiated unity in the self. It is more accurate to speak of the internalization of polarities or the compresence of dualities.[47]

Drawing on biology, psychology, and theology, essentialists present a convincing case that sexuality is fundamental to human nature and identity and is not simply some "extra" factor added onto a more fundamental human nature. Essentialism also points us toward the many ways in which sexuality is grounded in the biological givens of life. Despite our Enlightenment emphasis on the self-created and autonomous individual, who can become anything he or she wants? Essentialism forces us to realize that much of who we are results from the bodies with which we are born.

At the same time, we need to be careful with essentialist understandings of gender given the proclivity that we have for understanding our experiences and cultural perspectives of sexuality as universal norms about what it means to be male and female. Even if we affirm that sexuality is essential to human nature, we must be careful about thinking that we know what it means to be sexual. The sexual nature of the human person connects to the mystery of the human in many ways, as we will see in the next section. Consequently, the safest approach here may be to affirm a modest or chastened essentialism that acknowledges the fundamental nature of sexuality but declines to claim that it has fully grasped precisely what that means.

Finally, constructivism, helps us realize that the "givenness" of sexuality is not a biological reality alone. Instead, our sexuality is also given to us by the cultural context in which we develop as gendered beings. Indeed, constructivism presses us to consider the fact that even the apparently objective facts of biology are themselves influenced by cultural considerations. Our very bodies are shaped by this context, as well as the ways in which we experience and interpret our embodied selves. Thus, constructivism helps us realize that human sexuality is a far more complicated reality than we might first appreciate and that the obvious differences between men and women may not be as objectively real as they first appear. Indeed, it is the cultural variability of gender and its complex relationship to these variables that provides gender its flexibility, its ability to take on significantly different shapes in different contexts. "It is this amazing plasticity . . . that discredits much of what has been said about the difference between men and women. Although it is still as true as ever that men and women are sexually different from birth, this difference is also a function of the roles assigned to the sexes in a given society and culture."[48]

A thoroughgoing constructivism that depicts human sexuality as a social construct "all the way down," however, must be rejected. We have already discussed a number of reasons for thinking that human sexuality is more fundamental than such an approach would suggest. In the next section, we will explore a more explicitly theological perspective on sexuality that will also demonstrate that sexuality is an essential aspect of human existence.

The gendered existence of human persons, then, is a complex reality that is difficult to capture in a simple definition. Biology and culture work together to produce gender in a complex spiral of mutual interaction—one's biology providing the genetic structure but in turn being influenced by cultural perceptions and expectations. We can thus affirm both "that biology is a factor in shaping human identity" and that "our social location plays an equally important role in the formation of our identity."[49] The complex interaction of these factors means that although there are differences between men and women, the precise nature of these differences defies simple explanation. Some of the data suggest that there is an "innate" aspect to gender that results in certain gendered "tendencies and predispositions,"[50] but it is seldom possible to identify differences with their corresponding biological causes confidently. We should not be surprised by this. As one researcher points out, "In a complex, interacting, dynamic, causal system . . ., is it ever possible to partition the causes of any particular gender-related behavior exclusively into one of two simple and mutually exclusive categories: nature or nurture? The answer . . . is, probably not."[51]

Hopefully we have now developed a better understanding of the complex reality that is human sexuality and some of the biological and cultural factors that go into its development. Our study of gender must press on to consider another dimension of sexuality, however, before it is complete. If human sexuality is a fundamental aspect of human existence, and if human persons are basically theological beings who can be understood only in terms of their relationship to God (as argued in the previous chapter), then we must consider how human sexuality itself should be understood theologically.

HOW SHOULD WE THINK ABOUT GENDER THEOLOGICALLY?

We have not understood the human person fully until we have understood the human person theologically. That was one of the key insights of the previous chapter. What would a theological perspective on human sexuality look like? Although we cannot hope to develop a complete answer to that question here, we can explore some of the options and begin to get a sense for what the shape of such an answer might be.

a. Options for thinking theologically about sexuality

Sexuality as procreation

For some theologians, human sexuality is fundamentally about procreation and does not express something that is distinct to human persons. Thus, the declaration that God will create humanity as "male and female" immediately precedes the command to "be fruitful and multiply" (Gen. 1.28). Sexuality serves to ground reproduction. Because other animals are also commanded to reproduce (Gen. 1.22), sexuality and reproduction are aspects of humanity that express our commonality with the rest of creation.

As we saw earlier, this reproductive focus has been prominent in androgynous approaches to humanity, with some theologians seeing it simply as God's way of dealing with the eventuality of sin. More commonly, theologians reject androgyny but still see sexuality as fundamentally about procreation. Thus, for Augustine, "The union . . . of male and female for the purpose of procreation is the natural good of marriage;"[52] human sexuality is created for the express purpose of procreation.[53] The Catholic Catechism takes a similar approach, arguing that God unites man and woman in marriage "in such a way that, by forming 'one flesh,' they can transmit human life."[54] From this perspective, then, human sexuality is a biological reality given primarily to enable human procreation.

Although this perspective helpfully points out that sexual reproduction is something that humans share in common with other animals, it fails to account for the fact that the creation narratives actually mark human sexuality as distinct in important ways. First, we should recognize that although both humans and other animals are commanded to "be fruitful and multiply," only humans are explicitly said to be "male and female." This at least raises the question of whether the gendered nature of humanity indicates something that transcends mere biological reproduction. Thus, according to Stanley Grenz, "The narrator does not appear to view sexuality as simply a biological phenomenon limited to procreation, which humans share with the animals. On the contrary . . ., by designating only humans as male and female, the narrator attributes sexuality solely to humankind."[55] This has suggested to many that even though we would not want to deny the connection between human sexuality and procreation, there may be an added dimension to human sexuality that transcends this merely biological perspective. Second, the connection between sexuality and the *imago Dei,* which we will explore shortly, similarly presses us to look beyond the merely procreative function for our understanding of sexuality.

Another problem with this procreative emphasis is that identifying sexuality and procreation in this way implies either that many people are not fully human or that sexuality is not a fundamental aspect of human existence. A significant number of human persons are not capable of sexual procreation. What do we say about the young, the old, and those who for various reasons are not physically capable of procreation? More important, what can we say about the full humanity of Jesus? If sexuality is integral to human existence and if sexuality is fundamentally about procreation, it would seem that Jesus and all those who do not participate in procreation are somehow less than fully human. The only apparent alternative here would be to deny that sexuality is fundamental to being human. Instead, it is a secondary, although important, expression of a more fundamental humanity. We have already seen, however, that there are good reasons for rejecting such an understanding of sexuality. The procreative approach, then, stands in need of supplementation to explain how procreation can be viewed as an important aspect of what it means for human persons to be sexual beings while recognizing that there must be more to the picture than this.

Sexuality as fecundity

Thus, some look beyond procreation to the fecund nature of God as providing a theological perspective on sexuality. On this view, God himself is a naturally creative being who produces "offspring" (i.e., creation) as an expression of his very nature, and humanity manifests this divine fecundity through its sexuality. This takes place in its most basic form as sexual reproduction but overflows as well into all aspects of human existence in which humans express themselves through creative production (e.g., art, culture).[56] In this way, human sexuality is seen to be distinct from other creatures in that it manifests more fully and creatively the fecund nature of God in the world.

What is not clearly explained by theologians opting for this solution is how sexuality is connected to the myriad forms of human creativity that are understood to express the divine fecundity. Certainly we do not need to be sexual beings to paint, write, or sing. This perspective would seem to make fecundity the fundamental characteristic of being human, leaving sexuality to serve merely as one of many expressions of this more basic reality. Any such approach, however, again runs up against the problem of explaining the fundamental importance of sexuality for understanding humanity and the uniqueness of human sexuality in the biblical narratives.

In addition, we might raise some concerns about this approach from the nature of God. Divine creation is about more than God's fecund being. God does not create as a necessary expression of his divine being, as though all creation were a mere emanation of the divine self. Instead, God creates as a free expression of his all-encompassing love. However we understand the eternality of the divine will, we must understand his act of creation as an act of free self-determination. Consequently, although the act of creation was fitting to his character as a creative God, it must be understood from the perspective of divine freedom and love. Incorporating the notions of procreation and fecundity into our discussion, then, requires that we consider more closely the role of freedom and love in human sexuality.

Sexuality as marriage

At this point, many turn to the institution of marriage as providing the meaning of human sexuality. Looking at the creation narratives as a whole, the "male and female" of Genesis 1 climaxes not in reproduction but in the "one flesh" of Genesis 2 and the introduction of the marital relationship. Unlike the procreation view, however, this marital relationship is not just about reproduction—the narrative says nothing about the "one flesh" union producing offspring—but actually expresses a more transcendent truth, a truth about the nature of God himself. Thus, marriage unfolds as a key metaphor for understanding the nature of God. God appears in the Bible several times as a husband whose wife is alternatively Israel (Isa. 54.5) and the church (Rev. 21.2). Indeed, the key metaphor of Hosea portrays God as a husband who has been betrayed by the infidelities of unfaithful Israel. Paul makes this connection even more explicit, arguing that the male/female marital relationship is a revelation of the "profound mystery" that is Christ's love for the church (Eph. 5.25–32). At the very least, then, marriage becomes a creaturely picture of the faithful love of God. Many theologians contend that the marital significance of human sexuality reveals even more, manifesting a truth about the nature of the immanent divine being itself. Just as marriage comprises the bringing together of multiple persons in one intimate union, so the triune godhead constitutes an intimate joining of three persons in one divine being. The two becoming one of marriage mirrors the three in oneness of the godhead.

This marital perspective improves on the first two in several ways. By emphasizing marriage as the key to understanding sexuality, this approach retains the idea that procreation is importantly related to sexuality. However, by rooting this in the freedom and love that comes with the covenant of marriage, it presents a more accurate picture of these divine realities. At the same time, the marital perspective improves on the procreation analogy by identifying something that is uniquely human. Although there may be other animals that exhibit patterns of lifelong mating and commitment that are similar to the marital practices of humans—once again we can see that even where humans are distinct they share much in common with other animals—we can still affirm that sexuality as expressed in the covenant of marriage is a uniquely human phenomena.

At the same time, we must recognize that a marital approach to sexuality still does not address the concerns that we raised above regarding the limited scope of this approach for understanding the broad range of human sexuality as we actually find it. Marriage not only fails to encompass the sexuality of the old and the young, but it provides an even more restricted scope than the procreational approach by eliminating from consideration those who are single and/or intentionally celibate as well as those who choose to express their sexuality outside the covenant of marriage. We could exclude this latter group from consideration by arguing that such expressions of sexuality are a sinful distortion of the divine intention for human sexuality. However, this does not seem to help very much. At the very least, the fact that human sexuality is routinely expressed outside of the martial relationship suggests that the marital approach alone is insufficient for understanding the breadth and depth of human sexuality as it actually exists in the world.

In addition, a marital perspective will have a difficult time maintaining the significance of human sexuality in our resurrected state, where we will no longer "marry or be given in marriage" (Mt. 22.30). As we have already discussed, we should not think of our resurrected selves as asexual or androgynous beings but as continuations and perfections of our existing and sexual selves. Precisely what role our sexuality will play in this eschatological state is something that we still need to consider. For now, it suffices to point out that the marital perspective entails the unsatisfying conclusion that human sexuality will not have any continuing significance in the resurrection.

Finally, the connection that some theologians draw between marriage and the divine nature is tenuous at best. Although the Bible makes a clear connection between marriage and God's love relationship with Israel and the church, we find no such connection with the triune relations of the godhead. Thus, although marriage might serve as an analogy of how God relates to his people, it is not at all clear how this approach grounds its claim that marriage manifests the immanent nature of God.

Sexuality as relationality
Consequently, other theologians have sought to ground human sexuality in something more fundamental than any of these other perspectives. For these theologians, a theological understanding of human sexuality begins with the affirmation that humans are essentially relational beings. Throughout Genesis 2, the human person is presented as a being in need of personal relationship for human life

to flourish as God intended. Sexuality, then, is portrayed as a response and solution to this need for relationality. Even more, this sexually grounded relationality, as we discussed in the previous chapter, is often connected to the *imago Dei*. Thus, Robert Jewett contends, "A theological statement on human sexuality must begin with the thesis . . . that to be created in the divine image is to be so endowed that one lives one's life in an ineluctable relationship with God and neighbor."[57] Understanding sexuality begins with understanding relationality as it manifests the triune God. Thus, according to Karl Barth, human relationality images God by repeating on a creaturely level the kind of personal relationships that exist between the Father, Son, and Spirit.[58] It is human sexuality that makes such relationality possible.

Unlike the first two accounts that tended implicitly to limit their understanding of sexuality in ways that excluded large groups of people, the relational approach presents a more all-encompassing view of sexuality. In this view, all human persons are essentially related to one another and to God, regardless of their age, status, physical capacity, or particular form of sexual expression (or non-expression). In each of these myriad forms, human relationality serves to manifest divine relationality in creation.

Nonetheless, this approach again runs the risk of minimizing sexuality as a fundamental characteristic of the human person. By making relationality the most fundamental aspect of human existence and the primary way in which human persons image God, sexuality again becomes a mere secondary manifestation of this more basic reality. If what is most truly human about being human is that we engage in meaningful relationships, it would not seem that we need to be sexed at all. One could argue that such basic human relationships as "friend" and "coworker" do not require that we be sexual beings. What, then, makes sexuality fundamental to relationality when so many important relationships are not obviously connected to sexuality in any way? Barth attempts to mitigate this concern by arguing that although many human relationships do not require sexuality, those relationships that do require sexuality (parent–child, husband–wife, etc.) are the most universal and fundamental of all human relationships.[59] Thus, although not everyone may be involved in a friendship or other nonsexual relationship, all human persons are necessarily sexual beings and are always already involved in relationships that are sexual by the very nature.

Throughout the human person's life, these sexual relationships continue to have the utmost significance and serve as the ultimate paradigm of human relationality. As Alister McFadyen argues, "Gender difference and relation is the paradigmatic case of structural distance and relation in human being. Although it is socially instantiated in a variety of ways, to exist as man or woman and as man and woman is the concrete and necessary form of all human existence, and it is the biblical paradigm for human life as co-humanity or community."[60] Thus, although not all human relationships are sexual, human sexuality serves as the most basic expression of this basic relationality.

Although it might well be the case that sexual relations are the most basic and universal of all human relations, we can still wonder whether this serves as an adequate explanation of the relationship between sexuality and relationality. Does this not still make sexuality a secondary expression of a more basically human reality? If we were to become nongendered in the resurrection, on this view, would we actually lose anything important about being human as long as we continued to participate in meaningful relationships? To the extent that this perspective suggests that we would not, it remains an inadequate understanding of what it means for God to have created human persons as sexual beings. At the same time, we can press on the relationship between sexuality and the *imago Dei* on this approach. Although these thinkers often contend that there is a close relationship between gender and imaging God, it is not clear that this is actually the case on their system. If it is in virtue of being relational beings that we image the triune God, do we really need to be sexual beings to do this? Once again, even if we affirm that sexual relations are a paradigmatic expression of the *imago Dei*, they remain nonessential.

The relational approach also implies a sublimation of human sexuality precisely in the extent to which it abandons the procreation and marital perspectives. We saw earlier that the advantage of these approaches was that they took seriously the significance of sexual expression and reproduction in their understanding of sexuality. Although we do not want to lapse into making these the basic perspectives from which to understand sexuality, it would seem rather odd to develop an understanding of sexuality that ignored its physical manifestations and expressions entirely. Yet many theological discussions of this subject focus so much on abstract relationality that the concrete physicality of human sexuality is lost. This can only lead to the conclusion that sexuality is merely the gateway to understanding that which is truly human.

Consequently, although there is value to the relational approach, its failure to explain more adequately how relationality and sexuality are connected, along with its corresponding inability to incorporate the insights of the other perspectives on sexuality, suggests that further reflection is needed. Is there a way of connecting these important insights about relationality to the concrete physicality of the sexual human being? As Alistair McFadeyn argues, the meaning of human sexuality transcends its concrete physicality through its connection to the *imago Dei*, yet it cannot be understood apart from its essential physical components.[61] The final category that we will consider arose as a way of explaining the connection between our physical sexuality and relationality in more depth.

Sexuality as bonding

As we have seen, the relational approach runs the risk of minimizing the significance of human sexuality for understanding human persons. Indeed, in that schema, gender-differentiated sexuality does not even seem necessary for being human.

Consequently, several thinkers have suggested that we need to press beyond merely viewing sexuality as a paradigmatic expression of a more basic relationality and seek instead to understand how there might be a more intimate connection between these two basic anthropological realities. For these thinkers, our sexuality is fundamental to relationality because it is our sexuality that creates in us most fundamentally a need for the "other" that causes us to seek the fulfillment that comes only through our relationship with the other.

On this approach, the sexually grounded need for relationality is clearly manifested in the second creation narrative. There we find the human person, Adam, experiencing the loneliness and isolation of the solitary individual. Although he is surrounded by other created beings, none is found that can satisfy his need. The nature of this need becomes clear, however, only when God solves the dilemma through the creation of a sexually differentiated counterpart who is of the very same nature as himself. This solution "discloses the fundamentally sexual character of Adam's sense of isolation and hence of his personal identity as an embodied creature."[62] In other words, it was Adam's very sexuality that created in him a desperate need to find completion in another human person.

Sexuality, then, reveals an openness within the human person that can be addressed only by someone who is both "other" and "same." That an "other" is required can be seen in that Adam's need could not be met by himself alone. That the need be addressed by someone who is also the "same" as Adam is seen in the fact that neither God nor the other animals were suitable to serve as a counterpart for Adam. Thus, the sexual human being finds within itself a desire for another in whom there is both difference and identity.

As Stanely Grenz points out, however, simply affirming the "openness" is insufficient. Human sexuality not only manifests the lack of the solitary individual but also drives the individual toward completion in the other. Human existence is marked by "a fundamental incompleteness or, stated positively, an innate yearning for completeness," both of which are necessary to understand human sexuality in its entirety.[63] Thus, in addition to affirming the importance of the openness to the other created by human sexuality, we should also talk about the drive toward "bonding" that seeks to address this basic need. "[A]s sexual creatures, the basic purpose of humans' existence is related to the dynamic of bonding."[64] This drive toward bonding is a drive toward seeking wholeness, connection, and solidarity that characterizes much of human life. Sexuality manifests a lack at the core of the human person that results in a persistent drive toward the human other in search of relationship and community. This drive toward bonding is seen in Adam and Eve coming together as "one flesh." Grenz argues, "Rather than procreation . . ., the narrator seems to have in view the idea that the awareness of personal incompleteness and the yearning for completeness ('for this reason') constitutes the dynamic lying behind the actions of 'leaving' and 'uniting.' Understood in this more fundamental manner, sexuality comprises or evokes the drive toward bonding, which in the second creation narrative finds expression in marriage."[65]

This drive toward bonding, then, forms the basis of the connection between human sexuality and the broader importance of relationality and community for humanity in general. Indeed, the bonding of human sexuality is "the first step toward the establishment of the broader human community."[66] By this, Grenz is not referring to the reproductive nature of sexuality but to the fundamental importance of this sexually driven move toward bonding for all forms of human community. "As sexual beings, humans are fundamentally incomplete in themselves. Human sexuality not only participates in this incompleteness but also spurs individuals to seek community through relationships. The drive toward bonding that is characteristic of human life constitutes the foundation for various expressions of human community."[67]

This then is how bonding serves as the link between human sexuality and human relationality in general. The drive toward bonding produced by human sexuality is "a first step toward the establishment of the broader human community."[68] Human sexuality reveals our incompleteness and provides the drive toward completeness, but this is a drive that finds expression in innumerable human activities. "The mystery of our sexuality is the mystery of our need to reach out to embrace others both physically and spiritually. Sexuality thus expresses God's intention that we find our authentic humanness in relationship."[69] Indeed, although this drive toward bonding in community has its ground in human sexuality, its ultimate human expression resides in the bonding found in the eschatological coming together of the people of God. This is the end toward which human sexuality is fundamentally oriented, and it is here that human community in its truest form will be fully realized. Rather that denying the essential importance of human sexuality in the eschaton, then, this approach affirms that "the eschatological community is a realm in which sexuality—that is, the dynamic of finding one's personal incompleteness fulfilled through relationality—not only remains operative but operates on the highest level."[70]

This approach also provides a more compelling account of how human sexuality images God. Although recognizing that God is not a sexually differentiated being as humans are, we can affirm that human sexuality mirrors something important about the divine nature. The drive toward bonding in community presents one apt picture of the three persons in Trinitarian relationship, although we should always be careful about making one perspective on the Trinity our sole vantage point for contemplating the divine mystery. From this perspective, we do not see the three persons of the Trinity as a single, undifferentiated, divine being or as a loose community of three autonomous individuals but as a unique expression of relationship in which the three are always already bonded together by their mutual drive toward the "other who is also same" in intimate community. This eternal drive of each toward the other in powerful expression of divine love marks the divine side of the analogy found in human sexuality. To this extent, then, we can say that the divine being is "sexual"—that is, in God we see the three persons who are both "other" and "same" eternally bonded in intimate community. In this way, the divine being is the eternal ground of the drive toward bonding that finds its most basic human expression in the male and female of human sexuality and its ultimate human realization in the eschatological community of God's people.

Finally then, we can see that this approach also has sufficient explanatory power to make room for the insights of the other perspectives. The reproductive and fecund nature of sexuality can be understood as expressions of this drive toward community. Indeed, for many early theologians, the creation of the human community is precisely the reason for which human sexuality was created in the first place.[71] Thus, these serve as important expressions of, rather than the basic essence of, human sexuality. Similarly, marriage can be understood as a basic—perhaps even paradigmatic—expression of this drive toward bonding in the present age. Although humans continue to be sexual beings in the eschaton and, consequently, continue to experience a drive toward bonding with the other, the marital (i.e., covenantal) framework of this bonding will be expressed in the eschatological community and its relationship with the triune God.

CONCLUSION

A theologically informed understanding of human sexuality cannot afford to move too quickly into questions of how the genders ought to be related to one another, what roles men and women should perform in the church or society, or the proper ways in which to express one's sexuality. These are important questions and must be addressed as we seek to understand how men and women ought to live in the world. Answering them well requires that we think long and hard about the nature of sexuality itself and its significance for being human. We certainly have not completed that task in this chapter, but hopefully we have opened some helpful avenues for further discussion.

CHAPTER 4

MIND AND BODY

Soul and body, body and soul—how mysterious they were! There was animalism in the soul, and the body had its moments of spirituality. The senses could refine, and the intellect could degrade. Who could say where the fleshly impulse ceased, or the psychical impulse began?

Lord Henry Wotton, in The Picture of Dorian Gray
by Oscar Wilde

As I sit in my chair typing this chapter, I am clearly an embodied, physical being. I have a spatio-temporal location (i.e., I am in my chair at this moment in time) and dimensions such as height, weight, and volume. At the same time, there seems to be more to me than just my body. I have thoughts, feelings, and other "inner" experiences that are difficult to equate simply with my physical body alone. Indeed, I even seem able to think of myself as something distinct from my body. I find myself talking about my body, as though it were something that I possessed and used rather than something that constitutes my own being. Sometimes, I even imagine scenarios in which I exist outside my body or continue to exist after my body dies. What does this all mean? Is my physical body all that there is to me? Or, am I really some nonphysical thing—call it a "soul" or a "mind"[1]— inhabiting a body for a while? Possibly I am somehow both a body and a soul connected in some mysterious way? Or, maybe there is some other way of understanding all of this. These are the questions that will face us as we seek to understand more deeply the nature of human ontology.

How we understand human constitution has important implications for a range of issues including, among other things, personal identity, consciousness, free will, and the relationship of human persons to other animals, as well as such issues as the beginning and end of human life, the dignity of the human person, the nature and process of salvation, and, ultimately, the fundamental nature of what it means to be "human."

The questions surrounding the best way to understand the constitution of the human person, however, have proved remarkably difficult. The first and most obvious reason for this is the sheer number of proposals under consideration. According to one estimate, thinkers have offered no less that 130 different views of human ontology.[2] We can alleviate this difficulty somewhat by restricting ourselves to the most influential theories, but this still leaves us with a substantial number to evaluate. Needless to say, this can prove a daunting task. A second challenge comes from the biblical data. As we will see, although the biblical authors had much to say about being human, they made no attempt to provide a philosophically precise account of human ontology that would generate a decisive answer to the questions proposed above. This presents the opportunity for significant diversity on our question, even among people appealing to the same biblical texts. The number of discrete disciplines that are involved in the discussion likewise complicates matters. Indeed, to do justice to our question, it would seem that we need to be well versed in (at least) the fields of exegesis, theology, philosophy, psychology, biology, physics, and the neurosciences. The impossibility of any individual gaining more than a basic familiarity with so many disparate disciplines leaves many with a feeling of irreparable inadequacy. This last challenge is complicated by the tremendous speed with which contemporary scientific developments are proceeding. The last three decades have witnessed incredible developments in our understanding of the human brain. Thus, although understanding human ontology is vitally important because of its broad range of implications, it remains one of the most challenging questions to address in a Christian anthropology.

THE MIND/BODY DEBATE: CONSENSUS AND DISAGREEMENT

a. Areas of general consensus

As with many discussions, our best starting point for understanding this particular debate will be to consider the main areas of consensus among Christian scholars working in this area. We can identify four such areas of consensus.

1. *Human persons are embodied beings.* Nearly everyone affirms that human persons are physical, embodied beings and that this is an important feature of God's intended design for human life. Thus, most biblical scholars agree that although biblical terms such as "spirit," "soul," "body," "flesh," and the like, appear at first glance to refer to "parts" of the human person, they actually should be understood as referring to the human person as a whole, albeit from different perspectives.[3] So, for example, "soul" does not refer primarily to the immaterial essence of a human person but to the whole human person as a living being. Similarly, "flesh" denotes not simply the physical shell of the person but the whole person as a creaturely being. Thus, although we will see that there are important differences in how scholars understand the nuances of these terms and the biblical ontology that underlies their use, both Old Testament and New Testament scholars agree that the biblical texts focus primarily on the human person as a whole, psychophysical being. Theologically, as we saw in the previous two chapters, the *imago Dei* and the creation of human persons as gendered beings, both signify the importance of the body for understanding humanity. Similarly, the incarnation and the resurrection affirm the essential goodness of the physical creation and the centrality that physical embodiment has for true human life.

This affirmation of human embodiment means that at least two theories of human ontology are widely regarded as biblically and theologically inadequate. First, *idealism*, which views the human person as a purely "spiritual" being, finds few supporters among contemporary thinkers. Second, classic or "Cartesian" dualism, which argues that the spiritual and the physical are two, fundamentally distinct, "parts" of the human person, while not denying the physicality of the human, is widely criticized for its apparent denigration of the body and its overly sharp distinction between the material and immaterial dimensions of the human person. The contemporary consensus, then, maintains that any adequate anthropology must affirm human embodiment in ways that idealism and Cartesian dualism simply are not able to do.

2. *Human persons have a real mental life that is important and efficacious.* Most agree that we must affirm the reality and significance of humanity's vital spiritual, mental, and emotional life.

Human persons have an "inner" dimension that is just as important as its "outer" embodiment. From this perspective, then, most Christian thinkers affirm that there are certain aspects of the human person that cannot be entirely explained in "physical" terms alone. Instead, they affirm that human mental life is a distinguishable aspect of human existence that must be accounted for in understanding such things as mental causation, free will, personal identity, and conscious experiences.

Consequently, the current consensus rejects any reductive theory of human ontology. Such theories understand human persons as *strictly* physical beings—that is, "mental" realities are actually identical and explainable as physical realities. The "mental" language that we use (e.g., thought, feeling, decision) can either be reductively explained in terms of the underlying physical events that cause them[4] or should be eliminated from our language entirely as stemming from erroneous ways of thinking about the human person (i.e., the so-called folk psychology).[5] Neither of these approaches finds much support among contemporary Christian thinkers.

3. *We should develop our understanding of the human person in dialogue with contemporary science.* We will see that various thinkers differ in how precisely their theories interact with contemporary science, often disagreeing on the particular role that science should play in informing and/or evaluating the various proposals, but there is widespread agreement that our understanding of human ontology should be informed to some degree by modern science; no theory can simply ignore these findings and operate in a theological or philosophical vacuum. Thus, all of the theories attempt to engage and provide some perspective on recent developments in neuroanatomy, neurophysiology, and the cognitive sciences, among others.[6] Although not every theory agrees that it can be invalidated by this scientific data, its adequacy or inadequacy will be established at least partly on the basis of how convincingly it can articulate a way of dealing with this information.

4. *We must be able to affirm an understanding of the human person that maintains personal identity through death and resurrection.* Finally, most Christian theologians affirm that our understanding of human ontology must be sufficient to affirm an understanding of personal identity that can be sustained through such a radical transition as physical death and resurrection. This again suggests that any radical

dualism, which might imply that the body is unimportant for true human life, or radical materialism, which would reject the whole discussion as yet another manifestation of folk-psychology, will be inadequate as a Christian anthropology. At the same time, this area of consensus raises some significant challenges as each theory tries to articulate an understanding of personal identity that is consistent with its ontological commitments while explaining how this personal identity can be sustained through death and resurrection.

b. The shape of the debate

Within the space provided by these points of consensus, we still find Christian thinkers divided on how to understand human ontology. At its most basic level, the debate continues to be shaped primarily by whether one affirms some form of *dualism*, according to which humans are composed of two distinct substances or *physicalism*, in which the human is viewed as an entirely physical entity. As we will see, however, there importantly different ways in which each of these can be formulated.

Substance dualism

Although some forms of substance dualism have been largely rejected by contemporary thinkers, newer approaches have modified and clarified these earlier formulations in several important ways, and such modern dualisms continue to be prominent candidates for human ontology. As a theory of human ontology, substance dualism in any of its various forms makes three basic claims.

There are distinct mental realm and physical realms. Substance dualists view it as simply evident that the mental and the physical realms both exist and must be taken into account in any discussion of human constitution. If we look at the human person, we can see that he has "mental" aspects (e.g., thoughts, intentions, volitions, experiences) and "physical" aspects (i.e., a body), and that both of these are real. Dualists will present some formidable arguments in favor of their position, but they also contend that this is simply the "commonsense" view that has been held by most people throughout history.[7] Indeed, many physicalists would agree.

The mental and physical realms are both fundamental. Furthermore, substance dualists contend that these realms are both fundamental and, therefore not *reducible* to anything more basic. That is, neither the mental nor the physical realm is derived from the other, but they both exist independently as fundamental constituents of the universe.

The mental and physical realms are ontologically distinct. Consequently, substance dualists affirm that these two realms are ontologically distinct—that is they can (at least) conceivably exist separate from the other. Indeed, the notion of separability is so strongly linked to substance dualism that many identify this as its defining characteristic.[8] As ontologically distinct entities, the mental and physical substances are capable of entering into causal relationships with one another. The soul possesses a peculiar causal relation with its body such that it is able to act directly upon the body and be acted upon by the body.

Cartesian dualism construed these two substances in such a way that their fundamental differences made it difficult to understand what relationship they could possibly have with one another. Most contemporary dualists, however, affirm a form of dualism that presents a more "holistic" understanding of human persons. These thinkers seek an ontology that maintains the basic commitments of substance dualism (i.e., two ontologically distinct substances that are conceivably separable) while still affirming the functional interdependence of the entire person. We can identify at least three prominent forms of this modern substance dualism.

Holistic dualism. Holistic dualism "affirms the functional unity of some entity in its totality, the integration and interrelation of all the parts in the existence and proper operation of the whole."[9] Thus, the human person comprises two distinct "parts," but these two parts are fully integrated and interdependent such that the organism as a whole functions properly only when both are working in intimate union. Although it remains conceivable that soul and body could be separated at death and that the person could thus survive physical death in the continuity of the soul, it would be a truncated existence limited by the loss of the psychophysical union.

Emergent dualism. Another approach that has recently received significant attention is the idea that minds and bodies are integrally related because minds are *emergent* entities—that is, mental substances emerge from properly configured physical systems.[10] Thus, William Hasker argues that we should view the human mind as something that is "produced by the human brain and is not a separate element 'added to' the brain from outside."[11] Such properties are emergent in that

> they manifest themselves when the appropriate material constituents are placed in special, highly complex relationships, but these properties are not observable in simpler configurations nor are they derivable from the laws which describe the properties of matter as it behaves in these simpler configurations.[12]

Although we will see that there is a form of emergentism that is broadly compatible with physicalist commitments, emergent dualism transcends this approach by arguing that what emerges from the physical substrate are not merely emergent *properties* but emergent *substances*. Thus, although emergent dualists argue for on ontologically deep relation between the mental and physical substances, once the mental substance emerges, it is a distinct substance that is at least conceivably separable from its physical counterpart.

Thomistic dualism. Finally, a renewed interest in Aristotelian and Thomistic ontologies has generated a number of proposals for understanding substance dualism in terms of the soul as the *form* of the body.[13] For Thomistic ontologies, all material objects comprise a material composite (i.e., the matter from which the person derives) and a substantial form, which determines the essential nature of the object. In the human person, the soul is "the substantial form . . . in virtue of which the matter informed by it . . . constitutes a living human body."[14] Thomists thus view the soul as "an individuated essence that makes the body a human body and that diffuses, informs, animates, develops, unifies and grounds the biological functions of its body."[15] In addition, Thomists generally agree that it is (at least) conceivable that the soul could survive the death of the body, although its existence would be sharply limited.

Arguments against substance dualism

Substance dualism has long been the subject of stringent criticism. Unfortunately, many criticisms of substance dualism focus almost exclusively on Cartesian dualism, failing to recognize the ways in which modern dualists have moved beyond Cartesian dualism in emphasizing the embodied nature of human life. Frustrated by this, Charles Taliaferro calls for critics of modern dualism to present "a fair-minded, reasoned case against dualism" that takes seriously "the ways in which a version of dualism may do justice to the unified nature of embodied life."[16] In this section, we will consider whether these newer forms are as successful against key criticisms as this claim suggests.

The dissimilarity argument. Because psychophysical causal interaction is part of the very definition of this type of dualism, questions related to the coherence of its account of mental causation are critical for determining its overall adequacy. The problem of providing an adequate account of the causal relationship between the mental and the physical, however, has long plagued substance dualism, especially in its Cartesian forms. How is it that when I formulate a volition in my nonphysical soul (e.g., "I am going to move my arm now"), this nonphysical volition causes a corresponding effect in my physical body (e.g., my arm moves)? Descartes infamously attempted to resolve this problem by locating such causal transaction in the pineal gland. This answer failed to convince anyone, however, and many have concluded that substance dualism is simply unable to provide any kind of adequate resolution to this problem.

The problem of mental causation, however, actually stems from a number of related arguments. Among the oldest and most frequently cited of these objections contends that dualism's account of the two substances renders them so fundamentally different as to disallow any possibility of causal interaction. Causality in the physical world seems to involve things like proximity, energy exchange, and so on. Yet these are precisely the kinds of things that nonphysical entities do not do—they have no physical location, and they do not engage in energy transactions with physical entities (at least on most accounts). They are simply "different" and, consequently, they cannot engage in causal transactions with physical entities.

Dualists reject this argument for at least two reasons. First, they are quick to point out that the differences in view could include fundamentally different kinds of causation—that is, "physical" and "mental" causation. As completely different kinds of causation, we should not expect mental causation to meet the criteria and expectations of physical causation. They are just different. Indeed, some will argue that mental causation is so different as to be ultimately mysterious. This should not trouble us too much, however, according to these thinkers because physical causation is basically mysterious as well. As we will see in the next section, physicalists have their own problems accounting for mental causation. Dualists, then, contend that all causal relations are inherently opaque and that their position is no more fundamentally mysterious than that offered by the physicalists.

Dualists also feel justified in rejecting this argument in that it fails to provide any defense for its basic intuition. As Jaegwon Kim, himself a physicalist, points out, "As it stands, it is not much of an argument—it hardly gets started; rather, it only expresses a vague dissatisfaction of the sort that ought to prompt us to look for a real argument. Why is it incoherent to think that there can be causal relations between 'diverse substances?'"[17] The other arguments that we will consider, then, seek to provide exactly such an explanation for why dualistic causation is either incoherent or, at least, improbable.

The causal-pairing argument. The causal-pairing argument contends that dualistic causation is incoherent because it cannot provide any explanation for the causal relation that obtains between souls and the bodies.[18] In other words, what makes it the case that my soul interacts causally with my body and not the body of the person next to me? Causal relations in physical systems are typically established by "noncausal" properties such as spatial location, movement, and physical laws. Yet many thinkers contend that there are not any noncausal properties of a nonphysical, nonspatial soul that could account for its causal transaction with a particular body—it cannot be located *near* or *within* the body, and dualists cannot provide an account of the relevant nomological relationships that might govern such a causal transaction.

Once again, however, the modern dualist has a couple of responses. First, many modern dualists will repeat that mental causation is simply different from physical causation. Consequently, these will contend that mental causation does not need an explanation for this causal pairing—the body–soul causal relation is a brute relation and cannot be established or explained on any other grounds. Another response, however, recognizes the legitimacy of the objection for Cartesian dualism but denies that it is a problem for modern dualisms. The causal pairing problem seems to be a problem only if dualism entails that "we do not have the slightest hint of any relation holding" between souls and bodies.[19] But, many modern substance dualists affirm that the soul has precisely such a spatio-causal relation to a particular body and (it "emerges" from the body, it is the "form" of the body, etc.). Consequently, they avoid much of the force of this objection.

The principles of science argument. Many who object to dualist interactionism do so because of a conviction that modern science simply leaves no room for nonphysical causes of physical effects. These concerns stem primarily from a commitment to three basic principles:

> *Causal completeness of the physical* (CCP): Every physical event that has a cause at *t* has a physical cause at *t*.

> *Explanatory exclusion* (EE): "Two or more complete and independent explanations of the same event or phenomenon cannot coexist."[20]

> *Conservation of energy* (COE): The total energy of an isolated system remains constant regardless of any changes within that system.

These three principles constitute a significant challenge for substance dualism. CCP proposes that all physical events have physical causes. Thus, a physical event, like my arm rising, must have a physical cause, like the chain of neurons firing that cause the muscles to contract and my arm to rise. According to EE, however, if a physical event has a physical cause and, consequently, can be fully explained as a result of that physical cause, no other explanation is necessary; indeed, all other possible explanations are excluded. Thus, if I can explain the physical event of my arm rising by looking to the sequence of physical causes taking place in my physical body, I cannot also appeal to some nonphysical entity as an "additional" explanation of that event. Taken together, then, CCP and EE entail that all physical events have physical causes and that all physical events, therefore, can be fully explained in terms of their physical causes.

Once again, of course, the dualist could contend that mental causation is just different and does not need to adhere to these principles. Although CCP and EE might be valid *methodological* commitments for the physical sciences, we should not try to make them *metaphysical* theses. However, some have argued in rejoinder that this counter-argument misses the point of the physicalist objection. Physicalists do not merely criticize dualists for failing to maintain the physicalist framework but primarily for positing a theory than has little or no support from the physical sciences. Given science's superior explanatory track record, physicalists argue that we should assume a scientific framework unless and until it is proven wrong.

A dualist might fairly ask, however, what would qualify as proof in this argument? Because the framework of the objection rejects the possibility of nonphysical causes by definition, it seems unlikely that they would accept anything that transcended this framework. However, this predetermines the outcome. Thus, many dualists contend that the problem lies with the limited scope of these physicalist laws, rather than with dualism itself. This does not mean that modern dualists reject science; indeed, many of them rely heavily on the sciences for informing their understanding of how the psychophysical relationship works. However, unlike thinkers who affirm that science is "all-competent,"[21] dualists often contend that science is inherently limited in its ability to speak to the existence and nature of the soul.

A second response, however, notes that the physicalist solution is itself untenable. As we will see, both reductive and nonreductive forms of physicalism struggle to explain mental causation in a way that maintains its commitment to these basic principles while affirming the causal significance of the mental. Many dualists simply contend that given a choice between the two, the dualist framework is superior in terms of its ability to affirm the causal efficacy of the mental and the free agency of the human person.

The third principle, COE, likewise raises some problems for many thinkers.[22] Dualist interaction entails that mental substances are able to cause changes in physical systems. However, because physical causation requires energy transaction, any such change seems to entail a change in the total energy of the physical system, thus apparently violating COE, a fundamental law of modern science.[23] Dualists have offered two kinds of response to this concern. The first is to contend that COE should be understood as a statistical principle and that mental causation would not constitute a violation of COE so long as mental acts only involved small amounts of energy.[24] Thus, as long as the total energy of the physical system remains *largely* unchanged, COE does not constitute a problem. However, even if individual mental acts only involve small amounts of energy, the tremendous number of mental acts occurring on a regular basis would certainly constitute a statistically significant contribution to the overall state of the system. A second response argues that science only entails a weak form of COE—one that holds only for closed systems.[25] Psychophysical causation, therefore, does not violate COE because mental substances lie outside the physical system. Although it is certainly correct that psychophysical causation would not violate a weak form of COE, this approach does not take into account the physicalist's most likely rejoinder—(1) the lack of evidence for any mental substances outside the physical system and (2) the weight of evidence that the total state of energy of the physical system does not change both support the conclusion that a strong form of COE is justified even if not logically required.

It would seem, then, that once again the dualist's best response is to argue that psychophysical causation is simply different than physical causation.[26] In other words, because mental causation differs from physical causation, there is no reason to suppose that mental causation requires the transfer of energy. Even though physical-to-physical causation always requires the transfer of energy, it is not necessary to conclude the same for mental-to-mental or mental-to-physical causation. Although the physicalist will certainly not be convinced by this argument, it is logically consistent with the dualist's own framework.

The individuation and "other minds" arguments. Two other problems often raised against Cartesian dualism do not seem to be as difficult for modern forms of dualism. One classic argument contends that dualism has no way of individuating one soul from another. Because Cartesian souls are understood to be nonphysical, they cannot be individuated like physical entities based on spatial location.[27] Contemporary dualists, however, insofar as they argue that souls do have spatio-causal relations to particular bodies, should be able to utilize that as the basis for individuating between particular souls as well.

Finally, since dualism affirms a non-physical substance that is unavailable to empirical observation, many contend that dualism entails that human persons can only be confident in their own mentality and must remain agnostic with respect to the existence of other minds. In other words, whether the person across the table is actually a zombie with no mental life at all is something we can never know confidently. This argument, though, is routinely dismissed by dualists, who argue that even though dualism entails that we cannot have indubitable knowledge of other people's mental states, this does not entail that we must, therefore, be skeptical about their existence.

Physicalism
Physicalism comprises an entirely different approach to understanding human persons, viewing them as completely physical beings

(i.e., comprising no additional non-physical or spiritual substance) whose "inner" dimensions (e.g., beliefs, desires, intentions, feelings) must be understood in terms of their physical bases. Thus, although Christian physicalists reject any form of physicalism that dismisses mental realities entirely or views them as reductively identical with physical realities (i.e., "strong" physicalism), they are actively exploring physicalist ontologies that maintain a commitment to the reality and significance of the human person's "inner" life (i.e., "weak" physicalism).

Weak physicalism can be developed in a number of different ways. Each of them, however, tends to affirm five basic concepts:

The universe comprises a hierarchy of distinguishable "levels." According to many philosophers, the various entities in the universe, and the sciences that study them, are best understood hierarchically. Thus, Kim describes the world as

> a hierarchically stratified structure of "levels" or "orders" of entities and their characteristic properties. It is generally thought that there is a bottom level, one consisting of whatever micro-physics is going to tell us are the most basic physical particles out of which all matter is composed (electrons, neutrons, quarks, or whatever). And these objects, whatever they are, are characterized by certain fundamental physical properties and relations (mass, spin, charm, or whatever). As we ascend to higher levels, we find structures that are made up of entities belonging to the lower levels, and, moreover, the entities at any given level are thought to be characterized by a set of properties distinctive of that level.[28]

We have a picture, then, of the world built up of multiple layers, each of which is ontologically dependent on the layer below it.

The "mental" cannot be reductively understood in nonmental terms. This construal of the "levels" of reality, means that higher levels can never be exhaustively understood or explained based on lower-level concepts and theories alone. Unlike strong physicalism, weak physicalism contends that it is not only impracticable to talk about higher-level realities in lower-level terms but that something significantly new actually takes place on each level that makes it simply impossible to describe reductively these new levels of reality solely on the basis of the lower levels. Thus, although each higher level continues to be ontologically dependent upon lower-level realities, they must be understood on their own terms.

Human persons are fundamentally material beings. As a physicalist theory of ontology, weak physicalism continues to maintain a commitment to ontological monism. Consequently, it rejects any appeal to nonphysical substances as an explanation of human ontology. To flesh this out a little further, we can define physicalism as the theory that (1) human persons are either themselves physical entities or exhaustively composed of physical entities; (2) that all the properties of human persons are either themselves physical properties or properly related (whatever that proper relation turns out to be) to physical properties; and (3) that all causal processes are either physical processes or causally dependent on physical processes.

The "mental" is casually involved in producing physical events. Weak physicalists agree that mental processes, although they are ontologically dependent on lower-level realities, can exercise causal influence over lower-level realities (i.e., downward causation). Weak physicalists thus reject epiphenomenalism—the idea that mental properties are real but causally irrelevant—and dualism—with its affirmation of distinct substances. We will see that maintaining this tension between epiphenomenalism and substance dualism comprises a significant challenge for weak physicalism.

The asymmetric dependency of the mental on the physical. The hierarchical picture of reality drawn by weak physicalists along with their commitment to downward causation entails the concept of asymmetric dependency. That is, the levels of reality are somewhat interdependent, but because the lower levels are more ontologically fundamental, there is some element of asymmetry in the relationship. In this way the physical is accorded epistemological and ontological primacy but not ultimacy.

Weak physicalists often explain this asymmetric dependency using one of three different concepts. The first, *supervenience,* affirms that "mental properties or states of something are dependent on its physical, or bodily, properties, in the sense that once its physical properties are fixed, its mental properties are thereby fixed."[29] Thus, supervenience entails that higher-level properties or states (A facts) supervene on lower-level properties or states (B facts) if and only if (1) A facts are real (i.e., they are not merely conceptual); (2) A and B facts are distinct (i.e., they are not simply different ways of referring to the same properties or states); and (3) there is some objective dependency relationship between A and B facts such that A facts cannot change without a corresponding change with respect to B facts.

Although once quite popular, most philosophers now agree that supervenience ultimately fails to ground the asymmetrical dependency that it seeks to affirm. The concern is that supervenience merely establishes the necessary *covariation* of A and B facts without establishing either *how* or *why* this covariation takes place. However, covariation by itself is insufficient to ground a properly physical mind–body theory. What is needed is "a metaphysically deep, explanatory relationship" establishing the asymmetric *dependency* of mental properties on the physical.[30] Thus, while helpful, supervenience is insufficient by itself.

Consequently, weak physicalists, like some dualists, often appeal to the idea of *emergence*.[31] In a physicalist system, emergence refers to the conviction that higher-level entities exhibit novel properties that could not have been predicted and cannot be exhaustively explained by lower-level theories alone. This physicalist conception of emergence, then, is distinct from emergent dualism in that it does not affirm the emergence of a new substance. However, it does affirm that new properties emerge at each level of reality and that they cannot be epistemologically reduced. Two distinct types of physicalist emergence arise, however, with respect the causal efficacy of these emergent properties and CCP. *Emergent*$_1$ affirms CCP and maintains that the causal efficacy of the mental must be affirmed in such as way as to be consistent with this principle. *Emergent*$_2$, on the other hand, argues that once higher-levels entities emerge from their lower-level substrate, they exercise *autonomous* causal powers that are not fully determined by the physical causal framework.[32]

The third term, *constitution*, asserts that higher-level entities and properties are *constituted by but not identical to* the lower-level entities and properties that constitute them. For example, they argue that macro-entities, such as statues, dollar bills, and persons, are constituted by but are distinct from their copper, paper, and biological constituents. That this should not be understood as an identity relationship, according to constitution theorists, is established by the fact that such macro-entities have different properties than their constituent elements.[33] If you melted down a bronze statue and recast it in a new form, the statue would cease to exist, but the bronze would not.

Thus, it would seem that although the bronze constitutes the statue, it is not simply identical with the statue. In the same way, persons are constituted by, but are not identical to, their physical bodies.

Arguments against physicalism

As a theory of human ontology, physicalism faces its own important criticisms. As we noted earlier, many thinkers affirm that substance dualism is the "commonsense" understanding of the human person. This, of course, does not actually constitute an argument in favor of dualism because our commonsense notions might well be wrong. Many thinkers, including nondualist philosophers, however, agree that this commonsense intuition does place the burden of proof on physicalism.[34] In addition, nonphysicalist philosophers utilize a number of key arguments against the coherence of weak physicalism.

The consciousness argument. Probably the most common argument against physicalism is that mental entities involve certain properties that simply cannot be coherently explained in a physicalist system. Most commonly, critics contend that human mentality is characterized by *phenomenal consciousness*—that is, the qualitative *feel* that we associate with certain mental experiences. In other words, there is something that it is like to experience the taste of an orange, the sight of a sunset, or the feeling of a headache. Although fruits, sunsets, and pains are all physical things, my *experience* of them does not seem to be so. Accounting for these *qualia* (i.e., properties of phenomenal experiences) has long been regarded as one of the most significant problems for any physicalist ontology. How is it that "brain processes, which are objective, third person biological, chemical and electrical processes produce subjective states of feeling and thinking?"[35] It does not seem conceivable that there is anything it is like to be an atom or a chemical process, so how does it come about that organisms solely constituted by atoms and chemical processes are characterized by vital subjective lives? There seems to be an "explanatory gap" between our subjective experiences and our ability to explain them.[36] For many thinkers, this is the "hard problem" in philosophy of mind. Can we explain how a physical universe can give rise to subjective qualities?

Consistent with their framework, weak physicalists generally affirm the reality of such properties. They contend that humans have a real mental life that is characterized by such properties as intentionality and phenomenal consciousness and that these properties cannot be reductively explained on the basis of nonphenomenal properties alone (*contra* strong physicalism). Nevertheless, they contend that we do not need to appeal to distinct, nonphysical substances to explain the existence of these properties (*contra* dualism). One way in which the weak physicalist might do this would be to contend that the physical universe actually does have a phenomenological character at its core.[37] The very building blocks of the universe (whatever those might be) have within them at least the potentiality for phenomenal experiences. This kind of "naturalistic dualism" has received little support, however, given the lack of evidence for this theory and the apparent oddity of affirming that an atom can (even potentially) "feel" in any way.

A more common approach appeals to the principle of emergence to contend that phenomenal properties are exactly the kinds of unique properties that we should expect to find as we move up to the higher levels of the universe. Many will argue that this is similar to what we see in the concept of "life" itself. There is nothing about the non-living matter of the physical universe that would lead us to believe that it could produce living beings. Yet everyone now concurs that life is the direct result of combining non-living elements in certain ways. Similarly, these theorists argue, phenomenal properties are emergent properties derived from nonphenomenal matter.

Finally, taking a page out of the dualist playbook, a number of physicalists simply contend that phenomenological consciousness lies beyond our ability to explain.[38] Thus, although our commitment to physicalism entails that we must affirm the ultimate physicality of phenomenological consciousness, we may never be able to provide a satisfying physical explanation of it.

The conceivability argument. Another classic argument used to refute physicalism is based on the contention that if it is possible to think about the separation of the body and the soul, then they are conceptually distinct and, consequentially, nonidentical. This "modal" argument, moves from conceivability to metaphysical possibility and can be summarized roughly as follows:

Let "A" refer to me and "B" to my body.

1. A is B.
2. Given the indiscernibility of identicals, it is not conceivable that A can exist without B or that B can exist without A.

3. But it is conceivable that A can exist without B, and B can exist without A.
4. Therefore (1) is false; it is not the case that A is B.[39]

The first premise is established on the basic ontological commitments of physicalism.[40] The validity of the second premise is based on the principle of the indiscernibility of identicals; since the two are identical, it is not conceivable that one could exist without the other. The third premise, though, contends it is conceivable that I can exist independently of my body. This is usually established on the basis of thought experiments like mind-transfers, life after death, and out of body experiences. If it is conceivable that I could exist without my body, however, then it is conceivable that A is not B. Again, given the indiscernibility of identicals, if it is conceivable that A is not B, then A is not B.

The literature on modal arguments in general and this form in particular is quite extensive and lies beyond the scope of this chapter.[41] We will have to content ourselves with noting that the primary physicalist response is to deny the validity of (3). Physicalists will often contend that (3) is either untrue—it is not really possible to conceive of a person without a body, or it is based on faulty ways of thinking—we can only conceive of A and B being separated because we have misunderstood what A is. Either way, the success of the modal argument is based on faulty convictions about what it means to be human. Ultimately, then, the modal argument does a better job of identifying ways in which dualists and physicalists differ in their basic convictions and intuitions than of providing the indubitable logical critique of physicalism that it claims.

The mental causation argument. Given the objections to dualist mental causation in the previous section, it is perhaps ironic that mental causation also constitutes a primary objection to physicalism. Unlike the dualist problem of accounting for the causal interaction of two disparate substances, weak physicalism bears the burden of establishing the causal relevance of mental properties in a physical universe. This becomes critical when we realize that some account of such causal relevance seems necessary for grounding personal agency, moral responsibility, and rational mental processes (more on this in Chapter 5).

One key form of this argument contends that weak physicalism is unable to provide an account of mental causation without violating its own ontological commitments. Carsten Hansen helpfully summarizes the main steps in this argument as follows:

1. Suppose that a mental property instantiation M causes $P*$.
2. M has a physical supervenience base P.
3. On the standard accounts of causation, P qualifies as a cause of $P*$.
4. Mental properties are not reducible to physical properties.
5. M and P are distinct (simultaneous) sufficient causes of $P*$.
6. Overdetermination is unintelligible.

Conclusion: Mental-to-physical causation is unintelligible given nonreductive physicalism.[42]

To understand this argument, suppose that I am a weak physicalist, and I contend that my mind formulates a volition that causes my arm to move. Of course, as a physicalist, I also affirm that this volition itself has its own physical base. Combine this with a commitment to CCP, and it would seem that the physical base of that volition itself qualifies as the cause of my arm moving. Because I am a weak physicalist, the volition is not reducible to its physical base. It would seem, then, that I am affirming that the volition *and* its physical base *both* cause my arm to move. The idea that there can be two simultaneous and sufficient causes of the same event, however, is either incoherent or, at best, unnecessary. Thus Jaegwon Kim, the most prominent proponent of this argument, concludes that best way to account for mental causation in a physical world is either to affirm that the volition and the physical state are simply identical (reductionism) or that the volition is not causally relevant (epiphenomenalism).

Weak physicalists have offered three general responses to this argument. The first approach contends that the entire argument is invalid because it would ultimately undermine all higher-level properties and invalidate the sciences that study such higher-level realities (e.g., psychology, sociology). Consistently applied, then, the argument reduces everything to physics. This argument, however, simply points out the implications of the exclusion argument, without really providing a decisive argument for rejecting it.

Theists will often contend that if we affirm the possibility of divine action in the physical universe, then we have grounds for affirming that not all physical events have sufficient physical causes. This argument does not seem to be of much assistance to the physicalist, however, insofar as he or she does not want to portray the mental as a substance distinct from the physical realm, as would seem required by the analogy with divine agency.

Another set of arguments tries to construe mental causation in such a way as to avoid the implications of Kim's argument. One common approach has been to argue that when you are dealing with complex systems, like the human person, the entire system exercises causal influence on the behavior of its constituent elements. Although higher-level properties are ontologically dependent on their lower-level constituents, when they are combined into complex systems, they begin to exercise top–down causal efficacy with respect to these lower-level realities. Thus, the complex system that comprises human mentality can exercise top–down control of the lower-level physical system that comprises it. At the same time, the mental life of the human person is itself subject to top–down influence from higher-level social and contextual realities. It is, therefore, impossible to account for the behavior of any complex system in terms of its constituent elements alone; the system itself must be brought into the discussion as having an important causal role to play. Consequently, mental causes are not in competition with physical causes. Rather, they play a different role in the total causal process.

This argument, however, runs into at least one important problem. It is important to realize that, for the weak physicalist, no matter how high up in the system you go, higher-level entities are always asymmetrically dependent on their microphysical bases. If that is the case, any systemic influence these mental properties have is simply a larger part of the whole microphysical causal process. For example, suppose that some lower-level system has the potential to produce effects X, Y, and Z. Then, suppose that some higher-level system, s, acts on that lower-level system and causes it to activate Z from among those options. But s is itself asymmetrically dependent on its own lower-level base, b. As such, we can say that b causes s. Thus, even if we say that s causes Z, it does so only insofar as it is caused by b. At this point, we are left with the conclusion that even if it is helpful to appeal to s in our causal account of Z, we are simply putting a higher-level "label" on what is essentially a reductively deterministic process. If this is the case, mental causation is simply physical causation in disguise.

The personal identity argument. One final issue that has often been raised as a problem for any physicalist ontology deals with the continuity of personal identity. In a theological context, the question usually arises around the need to explain the continuity of personal identity through physical death and resurrection. Because the physicalist views the human person as identical to her body (or, nearly so, according to the constitution view), the human person cannot continue to exist separate from her body. If this is so, when my body dies, I will no longer exist. If God brings a bodily organism to life 2000 years later, what makes it the case that this bodily organism is me and not a mere replica of me? The question that emerges, then, is, "Under what circumstances is some person who exists at one time, *a*, numerically identical with something that exists at another time, *b*?"

Physicalists offer three general ways of understanding the continuity of the human person through time. The first response looks to *biological continuity* as the criterion for continuous personal identity. Thus, the body itself grounds personal identity. For these thinkers, however, "body" means more than a mere collection of physical parts, the persistent identity of which is notoriously difficult to establish. Instead, these philosophers assert material continuity in virtue of their understanding of the human body as a self-sustaining living organism.[43] On this view, two entities—*a* and *b*—are identical just in case *b* is simply a later temporal stage in a continuous biological organism of which *a* was an earlier stage.

A problem arises for such an account, however, when we consider the resurrection. If continuous personal identity requires the continuity of a living organism, how can you have any continuous personal identity *after* the death of the biological organism? One possibility would be to argue that the causal connections necessary for such biological continuity are able to cross temporal gaps such that *b* could be part of the same biological organism as *a* even though there was a time when the biological organism, of which they are temporal stages, did not exist. The possibility of such a temporally "gappy" existence, however, has been rejected by most philosophers as being incoherent within a physicalist framework. The primary alternative to such an account has been to suggest that although there can be no biological continuity beyond the death of the biological organism, it is at least conceivable that God could intervene at the death of the person so as to miraculously continue biological life despite the appearance of death. At least two different ways have been suggested for how God might accomplish this. According to Peter van Inwagen, God could create a simulacrum in place of the person's corpse, which God whisks away to be miraculously preserved until the resurrection.[44] Kevin Corcoran, on the other hand, suggests that a better, and less theologically disturbing, proposal would be to imagine that God copies a person's "simples" (i.e., the basic microphysical components of the human body) such that one set becomes a corpse and the second set continues the biological life of the person.[45] Either way, the basic premise remains the same. Despite the difficulties of establishing biological continuity, these thinkers argue that it is conceivably within God's power to intervene and sustain biological identity.

One could object, of course, that such proposals are highly sensational and speculative and that they have no ground in biblical texts or theological traditions. This objection certainly has some validity. At the same time, we must acknowledge that the resurrection is an essentially mysterious event. Consequently, we cannot expect any theory to do more than posit hypothetical examples of how an identity theory *might* be constructed. Thus, difficulties raised regarding the *believability* of a particular identity theory must be set aside in the face of something as inscrutable as the resurrection. We will focus instead on questions of coherence and adequacy. In addition, although we should be cautious with appealing to *deus ex machina* solutions to challenging problems, because the resurrection necessarily entails divine agency, we should assume that it is appropriate to invoke divine involvement to a certain extent.[46]

Other physicalists argue that what really matters is *psychological continuity*. Using thought experiments such as transferring a mind from one body to another or gradually replacing a human person's biological parts with entirely synthetic parts, these thinkers argue that the identity of the human person is most closely associated with her mental states and that even a total lack material continuity would not preclude continuity of identity. From this perspective, *a* and *b* are identical just in case there is mental continuity between them that is appropriately connected. On this view a theory of the resurrection could simply be constructed around the conceivability of God transferring the relevant mental states from one body to another.

A key objection to the psychological continuity criterion is the problem of duplication.[47] In other words, suppose that at the resurrection God decided to copy my relevant mental states twice and place these mental states in two different bodies. If psychological continuity is all that is necessary to ground personal identity, it would seem that both of these future versions of me would have equal claim to being me. Of course, the problem could be multiplied by supposing that God were to create thousands of different versions of me (a truly terrible prospect!) all with an equal claim to being me. There would seem to be no way of discerning which one was "actually" me.

The physicalist has a few options for responding to this concern. First, she could contend that identity is sustained only in cases where there is no such duplication. Any such duplication necessarily results in the loss of continuous identity. However, why should this be the case? Surely if mental continuity is sufficient for personal identity, it should still be sufficient even if the mental state is copied? There does not seem to be anything necessary to the simple fact of duplication that would render the identity relationship void. Second, our physicalist could argue that all we need to affirm is that there is significant *continuity* between the present me and the future me, strict *identity* is unnecessary. The Christian doctrine of the resurrection, however, requires a much stronger view of continuous personal identity. Surely it is important that *I* will be resurrected and not merely some being that has a lot in common with me. It is not at all clear, then, that psychological continuity alone will suffice to ground a theological perspective on personal identity.

Finally, some argue that there are no necessary criteria that ground personal identity.[48] This does not mean, however, that it is never possible to explain how *a* could be identical with *b*, it may in fact be possible to do this in many cases, but the *no-criteria solution* rejects the possibility that we could devise metaphysical criteria that would establish the identity of *a* and *b* in every case. Although we can affirm that identity persists, we will, not always be able to explain it.

This approach can be fleshed out in two different directions. One would be to concede that there are no strong criteria of identity and argue instead that identity is grounded in a person's first-person self-representation of a coherent narrative. Thus, present-me and future-me are identical so long as I understand myself in both cases to be the single subject of a continuous narrative. I would never be able to establish to a third party that future-me is the same person as present-me, there are no criteria that could do this, but I can be confident in my own continuous identity as the subject of the same story. Such an approach, however, leaves itself open to concerns about manipulation. Suppose that some evil scientist figures out how to completely wipe a person's memory and replace them with my memories. That person would now understand himself to be the continuous subject of *my* narrative. Because this approach maintains that there are no objective grounds for establishing personal identity, it would seem that he has an equal claim to being me simply in virtue of the fact that he believes it to be the case. This will not do.

A second way to approach the *no-criterion* solution, argues that although no single criterion is sufficient to ground personal identity, there may be some set of criteria that are jointly sufficient for that purpose. Physicalists opting for this approach contend that most people think of personal identity as comprising multiple aspects—including physical, psychological, and relational factors. Thus, my wife can have confidence that I am the same person at the end of the day as I was at the beginning of the day because of my bodily continuity (I did not change bodies during the day), psychological continuity (I have the same knowledge and memories as earlier), narratival continuity (I still understand myself to be the same person I was before), and even relational continuity (we stand in the same relationship to one another). Although none of them suffices on its own—I could be the same person even if I suddenly thought I was someone else—together they present a compelling case for continuous personal identity. A problem with this approach, however, is that if each of these elements can be individually challenged as providing an adequate account of personal identity, it is not clear that combining them really helps strengthen the case. In other words, if I have been convinced by the arguments above that the individual criteria all fail to establish personal identity, then it would seem that combining them would similarly fail; for example, God could create multiple beings who are biologically, psychologically, and narratively continuous with present-me. A combination of criteria might incline me to believe more strongly in someone's personal identity (epistemology) but it is no more likely to actually establish that identity (ontology).

c. The current state of the debate

Many contemporary philosophers believe that developments in the modern sciences have rendered substance dualism obsolete, such that dualism is no longer "a serious view to contend with."[49]

The ontological debate, however, is not so easily resolved. First, as we have seen, modern forms of dualism have been developed that offer new ways of interacting with the results of the modern sciences and responded to classic criticisms. Thus, instead of being eliminated by modern science, the vibrancy of modern dualism can be seen in the fact that the last several decades have witnessed a proliferation of nonphysicalist ontologies; for example, emergent dualism (Hasker), holistic dualism (Cooper), naturalistic dualism (Chalmers), integrative dualism (Taliaferro), and Thomistic dualism (Moreland) as well as other ontologies that do not fit easily into the physicalism/ dualism framework like idealism (Foster), pluralism (Cartwright), and Aristotelian hylomorphism (Nussbaum).

At the same time, there is a growing realization that although we now know more than ever about the nature and function of the human brain, we are still struggling to understand its relationship to human mentality. Thus, despite the progress of philosophy of mind and the cognitive sciences throughout the twentieth century, we remain limited in our ability to provide a theoretical framework for interpretation that information. As Steven Rose notes, "We are still data-rich and theory-poor."[50] We can see this theoretical limitation at work in the variety of ontological theories claiming the moniker "physicalism" and yet differing substantially in how human ontology should be understood—for example, nonreductive physicalism (Van Gulick), dual-aspect monism (Jeeves), constitutional materialism (Corcoran), and emergent monism (O'Conner) as well as the more reductive forms that continue to have significant supporters (e.g. Dennett, Churchland).

Thus, the debate about human ontology is still very much alive and well, with a number of important theories being offered on both sides. As Kevin Corcoran states, "the mind-body problem remains wide open."[51]

A WAY FORWARD: THINKING THEOLOGICALLY ABOUT HUMAN ONTOLOGY

The mind/body debate is an argument about the best theory for understanding human ontology; and, as we have seen, it is a debate with significant implications for a range of issues. Yet the Bible does not provide an indisputably clear perspective on this issue. Quite a number of studies have focused on the biblical material related to human ontology.[52] Unfortunately, the same physicalist/dualist debate that we find in philosophy and theology rages among biblical scholars as well. Although the majority of recent biblical scholars have argued in favor of a physicalist depiction of the person in the Bible,[53] there is no shortage of scholars contending for a more dualistic conception.[54] It seems unlikely, then, that the debate will be resolved at the level of biblical interpretation alone because the Bible just does not seem concerned with presenting a theoretically rigorous account of human ontology. Instead, it provides a theological *framework*, a way of thinking theologically about the human person, which has implications for what qualifies as an adequately Christian mind/body theory.

As we discussed in the opening chapter, any adequately Christian anthropology needs to begin with an understanding of human persons as *imago Dei* beings. Furthermore, orienting anthropology in this way has significant anthropological implications. We identified seven things that Christian anthropology needs to affirm about the nature of human persons: Christocentrism, relative uniqueness, mystery, relationality, responsibility, embodiment, and brokenness. These *imago Dei* affirmations, if they truly are central affirmations of a Christian anthropology, should be able to serve as key points in a biblical framework for understanding human ontology. In other words, any adequately Christian anthropology must be able to affirm each of these coherently (i.e., in a way that is consistent with its own ontological commitments). To the extent that any theory of human ontology is unable to do so, that theory must be viewed as less than adequate and, at least, in need of serious revision before it can serve as an aspect of a theological anthropology. On the other hand, any theory capable of coherently affirming these assertions, should be viewed as theologically adequate and worth pursuing more fully.

So, what happens when we apply this theological framework to the particular dualist and physicalist theories that we have discussed in this chapter? At least some of the affirmations seem entirely consistent (or, at least, potentially consistent) with both approaches. As we have seen, many dualists openly espouse the *mystery* of the human person, affirming that there is something about humanity that will always escape understanding. Physicalists, on the other hand, might seem more susceptible to criticism on this point since they view the human person as an entirely material being and, consequently, at least theoretically open to scientific explanation at every turn. As we have seen, though, weak physicalism affirms the emergence of higher level properties and complex systems with novel properties that cannot be comprehensively understood on lower-level terms alone. At the very least, the weak physicalist can affirm significant mystery at these higher levels. Indeed, given the complexities involved in understanding the universe at its most fundamental levels (e.g., quantum mechanics, string theory), many physicalists are willing to affirm mystery here as well.

Similarly, it might seem that each approach struggles somewhat with the *relative uniqueness* of the human person. Physicalist theories occasionally sound as though they have lost sight of the uniqueness of the human person, portraying humans as virtually inseparable from the rest of creation. Although this might be a necessary implication of strong physicalism, however, weak physicalism has no difficulty affirming that human properties are "emergent" in ways that set them apart form other animals. Thus, although there is nothing that separates humans from animals ontologically—we are all physical creatures—humans still exhibit "higher-level" properties, capacities, and behaviors that are unique in creation. Dualists, on the other hand, are often critiqued for losing sight of the relativity of human uniqueness, portraying the human "soul" and its capacities as completely without parallel in creation. Thus, many dualists have argued that only human persons have souls, sometimes going so far as to contend that other animals are merely biological machines. Nonetheless, modern dualists present a much different picture of human uniqueness. Many of these thinkers explicitly incorporate animal "soulishness" into their ontologies, with some affirming an evolutionary account of the human soul.[55] Both approaches, then, are able to affirm the relative uniqueness of the human person in creation, even if some forms of each press too far toward either extreme.

A second point, *Christocentrism*, raises more pressing questions. All of the theories that we have discussed are quite able to affirm that Jesus Christ should be the starting point for any adequate understanding of the human person. However, some have questioned the adequacy of a physicalist ontology at precisely this point. First, some have claimed that only a dualist ontology is capable of supporting an orthodox understanding of the incarnation. It is not entirely clear, though, why this should be so. Surely the mystery of the incarnation is sufficiently broad and deep to encompass either set of theories. As we have seen, though, a more significant challenge arises with the resurrection. The biblical narratives clearly portray Jesus as the same person both before and after the resurrection. Indeed, the soteriological significance of Jesus' death, resurrection, and ascension would seem to require that he be the same human person throughout. Yet we have seen that significant questions remain as to whether a physicalist ontology is capable of coherently affirming any such notion of personal identity.

In addition, despite the fact that many theologians from each perspective would affirm the significance of Christology for understanding the human person, neither approach has really engaged Christology in their own understanding of human ontology. Indeed, many seem more concerned about the implications that a particular theory might have for our understanding of Jesus than exploring how the person and work of Jesus should inform our understanding of human ontology. Unquestionably, more work needs to be done here.

Finally, each approach faces some important challenges with respect to *responsibility*. As we have seen, some account of responsibility is necessary to ground human relationality, moral accountability, and their role as *imago Dei* beings in creation. On most accounts, however, responsibility requires that human persons be able to formulate thoughts and volitions that are causally efficacious in the production of their actions. In other words, responsibility requires mental causation. Both dualism and physicalism, however, face serious questions with respect to their understanding of mental causation. The physicalist's account of mental causation seems trapped between its commitment to the causal completeness of the physical world and its claim that mental entities are real and causally efficacious. Thus, weak physicalist seems forced either to deny of one of these core convictions or to appeal to the existence of multiple sufficient causes for the same event (overdetermination). Because neither of these options is palatable to most weak physicalists, more work is needed to explain how weak physicalism can offer a coherent account of mental causation and moral responsibility.

Dualists, however, have problems of their own. Although modern dualists strongly affirm the integral relationship between the mind and the body in human life, in their account of mental causation, dualists frequently accentuate the fundamental differences between the mental and physical substances. Mental causation is often portrayed as ultimately mysterious and its connection with physical events as simply inexplicable. To the extent that they do this, however, dualists begin to undermine their own commitment to the psychophysical nature of embodied human life. If the connection between the mind and the body is entirely opaque and mysterious, how can we truly affirm that they are as tightly interrelated as the contemporary dualist claims? Here as well, more reflection is needed.

Thus, mental causation remains a problem for both accounts. As it is a problem for both, however, it can hardly constitute a decisive objection against either. Indeed, given the inherent difficulties in trying to provide an adequate account of causation in general, let alone mental causation, we should not be too surprised by these struggles.

This leads us to a final area, that of *embodiment*. Physicalism affirms the embodied nature of human life in very clear ways, sometimes to the extent that their account of personal identity becomes problematic. Dualists, however, have long been criticized for denigrating or, at least, devaluing the nature of the body. Although contemporary dualism goes a long way toward alleviating some of these concerns, more work needs to be done. We have just seen that the dualist account of mental causation seems to undermine their emphasis on embodiment. The dualist description of the state of the human person between death and resurrection is often problematic as well. All dualists affirm the conceivability that the mind (and, typically, the person) can continue to function, to some extent, independently of the body. Although most contemporary dualists contend that this would be a truncated existence, severely limited by the loss of the body, thus emphasizing the integrated nature of humanity's psychophysical constitution, their descriptions often suggest otherwise. On one account, "human persons in the interim state can be spoken of as having experiences, beliefs, wishes, knowledge, memory, inner (rather than bodily) feelings, thoughts, language (assuming memory or earthly existence)—in short, just about everything that makes up what we call personality."[56] If all of these things can function independently of the body, we must raise real questions about how seriously the embodied nature of human life is really being taken.[57]

CONCLUSION

What am I? Am I a physical thing? Am I a spiritual thing? Am I some combination of the two? Am I something else entirely? These questions continue to generate heated debate among Christian thinkers and are unlikely to be resolved in the near future. Indeed, at this point in the conversation, it is difficult to picture what a resolution to this issue would even look like. Our approach in this chapter, consequently, has been to find a way of thinking through the issues, rather than trying to resolve the debate itself. Thus, I have argued that what is most important in this discussion, is that we make sure that our understanding of human ontology, whatever it might be, is capable of sustaining the core affirmations that we need to make about the human person is order to have a theologically adequate understanding of humanity. An ontology that rejects any of these affirmations must be rejected as a viable option for an adequate anthropology.

Ideally, we are seeking an ontology that can affirm all of these things about the human person and do so in a way that is entirely consistent with its own ontological commitments. As we have seen, however, most of the options on the table struggle to provide coherent explanations of at least a few of these affirmations. As long as this remains the case, it would seem that our best course of action would be to hold any ontology on a tentative and provisional basis.

CHAPTER 5

FREE WILL

Man is the intersection of two worlds. . . . [I]n him there takes place the conflict between spirit and nature, freedom and necessity, independence and dependence.

Nikolai Berdyaev[1]

In our discussions of the human person, we have repeatedly encountered the notion of "free will" and its centrality for understanding what it means to be human. In this chapter, we will take up this issue in a more direct manner as we wrestle with what it means to affirm or deny that a person has or exercises "free will."

There are few issues in Christian thought that generate more problems and more visceral reactions on how we understand free will. This almost certainly stems from a realization that this concept stands at the heart of any adequate anthropology. How we understand the concept of human freedom touches on nearly every aspect of human existence. Most obviously it shapes fundamental moral concepts such as responsibility, accountability, personal development, and interpersonal relationality. Theologically, it affects our picture of the God–human relationship, the existence and nature of sin, the problem of evil, the nature of salvation, and the process of sanctification. Add to that its significance for understanding the mind–body relationship, as we discussed in the previous chapter, and the importance of freedom in social theory and political philosophy, and you begin to see how "free will" significantly shapes one's overall world view.

The free will debate is a long and complex one, with no easy resolution. Indeed, an adequate Christian perspective on this issue would require (at least) careful definitions of all the terms involved; a thorough consideration of the proper relationship between science, philosophy and theology; an exegetical analysis of all the relevant biblical data; theological discussions of key doctrines (e.g., doctrine of God, Christology, salvation, sanctification); and consideration of the relationship between factors "external" to the human person (e.g., divine decrees, natural causes, genetic inheritance, cultural conditioning) and "internal" factors (reasons, desires, character, etc.). Given the near impossibility of any one person gaining proficiency in all of these disparate fields of inquiry, an adequately comprehensive account of free will seems impossible. Nonetheless, we will seek in this chapter to establish some of the basic parameters of the debate, understand some of the key arguments involved, and develop a way of thinking about these issues that will help us develop a theological understanding of the human person as a free being.

THE FREE WILL DEBATE: CONSENSUS AND DISAGREEMENT

a. Areas of general consensus

1. *Human persons have free will.* A number of options have been proposed for understanding free will. Some have simply denied that free will exists in any meaningful form. According to such *hard determinism* free will is an illusion and the human person's decisions are fully determined by factors that precede them and lie outside the person's control. Most contemporary thinkers, however, reject such hard determinism and affirm the reality of free will. Although we will see that what is meant by free will differs tremendously from one thinker to another, Christian theologians unanimously affirm that human persons do in fact have free will. This is important to affirm at the beginning of our discussion. Given the different ways that free will is defined, there is a common temptation to assert that some group denies the reality of free will. That is not the case, even though we might find reasons to question the adequacy of some particular definition.

2. *Human persons exercise free will in meaningful ways that render them morally responsible for (at least some) of their actions.* The precise nature of free will and moral responsibility is itself debated. Nonetheless, we must recognize that all parties affirm that

any adequate view of free will must be adequate to ground moral responsibility. This means that Christian thinkers are united in rejecting *fatalism*. According to fatalism, there is some outcome that is a fixed and unchangeable reality; there is nothing that I can do to change the fact that this outcome will occur. Fatalism, then, says nothing about whether I have free will, but it does deny that my free will has any significance because the ultimate outcomes cannot be affected by my actions. Christian thinkers, on the other hand, affirm that free human actions are meaningful in that they can and do affect future events and in that we can be held morally responsible for both the actions and their consequences.[2]

3. *Not all human actions and decisions are meaningfully free.* Certain human actions are clearly not free on any definition of "free." When the doctor taps my knee and it reflexively jerks upwards, everyone agrees that this is not a free action. Thus, reflex actions and other purely involuntary actions cannot be regarded as free. Most would also include in this category any action that is the result of manipulation or coercion. Suppose that I have been brainwashed by some mad scientist into believing that all white bunny rabbits are evil and are trying to kill me. If he throws a white bunny rabbit at me in a locked room, most would affirm that any actions that I perform in response to that situation are unfree because they would be the direct result of external manipulation. All of the parties in this debate, then, agree that those actions that are most pertinent to the discussion are those in which the human person is clearly free (i.e., they are nonreflexive, voluntary actions free from manipulation or coercion).[3]

4. *Free will is compatible with divine sovereignty.* We must also recognize that all parties in the debate agree that God is "sovereign," and that humans have significant free will nonetheless. Although it is often argued that libertarians implicitly deny divine sovereignty, this simply is not the case. While libertarians would be inclined to define "sovereignty" somewhat differently than many nonlibertarians, they are often very explicit in their affirmation that God is the sovereign ruler of the universe and that nothing lies beyond the scope of his authority and power. How he chooses the exercise this power and authority, of course, is an entirely different matter.

5. *Free will is importantly related to antecedent factors.* Finally, all of the views that we will consider affirm that there are a variety of

things that precede (logically or temporally) a person's choice for or against a particular action—e.g., the person's own reasons, desires, beliefs, and character; more "external" causes like the person's physical environment; and theologically significant factors such as divine decrees and events directly produced through divine agency. We will see that each view differs from the others in explaining precisely how these antecedent factors are related to particular free will choices and actions; nonetheless, they all agree that these factors are important and must be accounted for.

b. The shape of the debate

The debate surrounding free will focuses on three key questions. *What constitutes a "free" action?* We can identify three main options for understanding what it takes for an action to qualify as a freely willed action.[4] First, we can say that an action is free when it is the result of *rational deliberation*—when the person chooses on the basis of his or her desires, beliefs, and values, or "rightly ordered appetites." Second, others will argue that some principle of *ownership* must be involved; that is, the action is only a free action when it is owned or properly related to the person in some way. Third, many will contend that even ownership is insufficient; an action is only truly free when it is under the *control* of the human agent in some meaningful sense. Each of these three principles—*rational deliberation*, *ownership*, and *control*—will play significant roles in the debate between the various theories of free will.

Are actions caused and, if so, by what? If we determine that some action of mine was a free action, what caused me to do it? Here as well we can identify three main candidates for answering the question. First, some will argue that free actions do not have causes. This *noncausal* approach contends that free actions are "basic" and are not produced by anything. As we will see, this approach has not generated much support, with most thinkers affirming that free actions are caused. The second, and most common, approach is to identify the cause of the free action as some antecedent event. On this *event-causal* approach, some (mental, physical, spiritual) event preceded and caused the free action. Finally, some contend that the event-causal account is insufficient for a robust notion of free will and that the only cause of a truly free agent is a free "agent." On this *agent-causal* account, the human agent himself or herself is the direct cause of his or her free actions.

Is this causation deterministic or indeterministic? The noncausal approach, of course, rejects this as a valid question. The other two more prominent approaches, however, must both address the nature of the causal relationship. A deterministic account of causation can be defined as follows:

> An event (such as a choice or action) is *determined* when there are conditions obtaining earlier (such as the decrees of fate or the foreordaining acts of God or antecedent causes plus laws of nature) whose occurrence is a sufficient condition for the occurrence of the event. In other words, it must be the case that, if these earlier determining conditions obtain, then the determined event will occur.[5]

Thus, some set of conditions *C* makes it the case that some event *E* comes about. It is deterministic in that given *C*, *E* necessarily results. It is hypothetically possible that some other event could have occurred had *C* been different than it was, but given the way that *C* actually was, *E* is the only possible outcome. The determining factor(s) in this account could be understood from a primarily naturalistic perspective (e.g., the antecedent chain of physical causes, environmental factors, genetics), or from a more supernaturalist perspective (e.g., God, the gods, fate). In either case, the antecedent conditions fully determine the final outcome.

Indeterminism, on the other hand, denies that a free action can be produced by an antecedent set of conditions sufficient for making it the case that the action would inevitably occur. This does not mean, of course, that no action can be deterministically caused in this way, only that no truly *free* action is.

Each of these questions—what constitutes a free action, what causes a free action, and what kind of causation is involved—shapes the discussion in important ways. The third question, however, typically serves as the basis for the most common way of organizing the various theories. Consequently, the discussion usually revolves around two sets of theories: those that affirm determinism even while maintaining the reality and significance of free will (compatibilism) and those that hold to some form of indeterminism (libertarianism).

Compatibilism

The first set of theories that we will consider are those that hold to two basic convictions:

1. All human actions are fully determined by antecedent causes.
2. Human persons are free and can be held morally responsible for their actions.

This approach, then, maintains that free will is fully *compatible* with the truth of determinism.[6] Compatibilists are well aware that there are ways of defining "free" that would make this position completely incoherent. They argue, however, that there are other, and better, ways of understanding "free will" that can be shown to be compatible with determinism.

Arguments for the truth of compatibilism tend to come from three directions. As we saw in the previous chapter, many argue that contemporary science has convincingly demonstrated that human beings are physical creatures and that all physical creatures are governed by the same causal laws. Thus, however we understand human free will, we must do so within the causal framework of the physical world.

Many also have strong philosophical reasons for affirming compatibilism. We have already seen that most thinkers reject hard determinism because of its unacceptable rejection of free will and the consequences that this has for moral responsibility. We will also see that many of these philosophers are also convinced that there are good reasons for rejecting libertarianism as well. As these thinkers have concluded, then, that it is not possible simply to deny free will (hard determinism) or to deny determinism (libertarianism), the likeliest remaining option is that it is possible to affirm both free will and determinism (compatibilism).

Finally, compatibilists often appeal to a number of key biblical and theological arguments supporting compatibilism. The Bible is quite clear that God rules sovereignly over all creations; nothing that happens lies outside his sovereign power (Ps. 103.19, 115.3; Prov. 16.4). Indeed, the Bible goes further and talks about God's eternal decrees and plans (Isa. 25.1; Job 2.29) that seem to encompass not only the major events in redemptive history (Acts 2.23) but even the apparently random details of life (Ps. 139.16; Prov. 16.33) and the choices of human agents (Gen. 50.20; Acts 4.27–28). Texts such as these have convinced many that God's decrees and plans do in fact constitute a set of conditions sufficient for determining every action of human persons. Thus, Paul Helm concludes, "Not only is every atom and molecule, every thought and desire, kept in being by God, but every twist and turn of each of these is under the direct control of God."[7]

As with any complex debate, compatibilist theories of free will have been explained in a number of different ways.

Classic compatibilism. The traditional approach to compatibilism contends that we should view an action or decision as free just in case the agent is able to do what he wants without constraint. On this view, unimpeded *rational deliberation* is what really makes an action free. Thus, my decision (*D*) to watch *Pirates of the Caribbean* (the first one, of course) was free because I wanted *D* and nothing prevented me from choosing *D*. *D* was fully determined, however, because given the antecedent conditions (e.g., my reasons and desires as well as the circumstances of my environment and/or the decrees of a divine being), there was no possibility that I would have made any other decision. Indeed, the compatibilist views it as absurd that I would have made any other choice in *exactly the same circumstances.* If I wanted to choose *D*, and if my rational processes led me to view *D* as the best way to get what I wanted, why would I suddenly (and apparently without explanation or cause) choose *E* instead? Lacking some constraint forcing me to choose *E* against my own desires and deliberations, it would appear completely random and, consequently, not a free action under my control.

This approach has been especially popular with theistic compatibilist. So, for example, Jonathan Edwards famously argued that one always wills or chooses in accordance with one's strongest preference or inclination.[8] Similarly, John Frame argues, "The root of human decision is the heart."[9] Human actions, then, are free insofar as they are legitimate expressions of the human person's desires. As a theistic determinist, however, Frame maintains that God "forms the purposes of the heart" and in this way "controls our free decisions and actions."[10] My decision for *D*, then, was both free (i.e., what I wanted to do) and determined (i.e., God determined that I would desire *D*).

As we will see, classic compatibilism has been rejected by most philosophers in response to a number of significant criticisms. Most important, classic compatibilism does not seem to address the problem of compulsive desires. What if my desire to watch *Pirates of the Caribbean*, is actually an irresistible compulsion that stems from a psychological disorder of some kind. Classic compatibilism would seem to portray this as a free decision because it stems from my own desires, but most would reject the notion that a compulsive behavior should be viewed as a free action. Thus, newer forms of compatibilism have been developed to address this weakness.

Hierarchical compatibilism. Among the most influential of these accounts, hierarchical compatibilism contends that an action is truly free when it expresses the deepest desires, or the true self, of the human agent. We act most freely when we act in accord with the self with which we most fundamentally identify. Daniel Dennett provides an example of this argument using Martin Luther.[11] At the Diet of Worms, Martin Luther stood up and declared, "Here I stand, I can do no other." Dennett asks us to take this statement quite literally— given Luther's character, experiences, and convictions, it was actually impossible for him to make any other declaration. Despite the fact that this was the only possibility—i.e., Luther's action was fully determined—Dennett contends that we would still view this as a free action and hold Luther accountable for it. Indeed, he argues that it would be rather odd not to. If the action is a true reflection of Luther's desires, character, and convictions, it would seem the perfectly reasonable to view his action as a free and responsible action. Thus, on this account, actions are free insofar as they are expressions of the person's deepest self.

What about the problem of compulsive behavior? Harry Frankfurt addresses this problem by positing a distinction between first-order desires (a desire for something) and second-order desires (a desire about another desire). For example, suppose that I have a first-order to lie to my wife that is produced by a compulsive lying problem that I have; but I also possess a second-order desire not to act on this first-order desire and tell my wife the truth instead. Should my compulsion prove too strong and I end up lying to my wife anyway, the hierarchical compatibilist would contend that this is not a free act because it is not in accord with my deepest and truest desires. It is only when I have the will I want to have, that I am meaningfully free.

Reasons-responsive compatibilism. Another contemporary form of compatibilism argues that actions are free actions when they are properly responsive to rational considerations. Presumably, when I decided to watch *Pirates of the Caribbean* I had good reasons for doing so. If so, then it would be the case that if I had other, more

THEOLOGICAL ANTHROPOLOGY

compelling reasons for watching *Amelie* instead, I would do so. The counterfactual possibility that I would have chosen differently given a different set of reasons demonstrates that my decision was "reasons-responsive" and, consequently, free. So, even if we affirm on the compatibilist account that, given all the antecedent circumstances, I could not have any other set of compelling reasons than I actually did, nonetheless, it is counterfactually true that I would have chosen otherwise had I had other compelling reasons and, consequently, my decision is sufficiently reasons-responsive to render it a free action. On the other hand, consider my compulsive lying problem. Because this is a compulsive behavior, even if I had other reasons for telling the truth, I would still have lied. Thus, my decision to lie was not reasons-responsive and was, consequently, not free.

Arguments against compatibilism

The consequence argument. The most prominent argument directed against any form of compatibilism has been the *consequence argument*. This argument can be summarized roughly as follows:[12]

1. No one has power over the facts of the past and the laws of nature.
2. The facts of the past and the laws of nature determine the facts of the future.
3. Therefore, no one has power over the facts of the future.

Accordingly, if the consequence argument is true, it would seem that no person has any control over how his or her own future will unfold. To see this, consider again my decision to lie. According to determinism, my decision, D, is determined by antecedent conditions, C. And, since C precedes my decision, there is nothing that I can do at the time that I make the decision to bring about a different result. Given C, D is inevitable. A problem arises, however, when we consider that I have no control over C. There is nothing that I can do at the time of my choice to change the antecedent physical or supernatural factors determining my decision. But, if I have no control over C it would seem that I also have no control over D. If I have no control over D, though, how can I be held responsible for it? In what way can it meaningfully be said that I freely brought about my decision to lie and should be held responsible for that action when in fact I had no control over that which led me to make the decision? How can

I be held to account for the *consequences* of an action over which I exercised no meaningful control? This *consequence argument* has convinced many that determinism fundamentally undermines free will and moral responsibility.[13]

Compatibilists have responded to this argument in two different ways. First, many compatibilists have attacked the first premise, that there is nothing the person can do to change past facts. Instead, these compatibilists argue that even though there is nothing *now* that I can do to change past facts, it is still possible that those past facts *could have been* different. Had those past facts been different, it is conceivable that I would have chosen differently than I did. As it is hypothetically possible that the past facts could have been different than they were, we can also speak of different possible futures. Thus, the consequence argument fails to establish that the human agent has no control over or responsibility for his or her future.

This hypothetical conditional argument does not seem entirely satisfying, however. For one thing, even if the argument succeeds, it does not change the fact that in the actual circumstances in which I find myself, there is nothing that I can do to change the antecedent circumstances or the fact that these will determine the future outcomes. More fundamentally, however, the conditional argument fails to address the problem of accounting for how the past facts could have been different given the fact that they were themselves determined by their antecedent causal conditions. Simply pushing the problem back in time is of no help in establishing how it can be said that one can change the past facts in such a way as to enable different possible outcomes. So, it does not seem that the first premise of the consequence argument can be easily avoided.

Many compatibilists offer a second response to the consequence argument. These thinkers agree that determinism entails the denial that human agents have alternative possibilities in any given instance, but they contend that this truth does not undermine moral responsibility. As this response overlaps with the next argument, we will consider it in more detail under that heading.

The alternative possibilities argument. Many contend that any meaningful sense of free will and moral responsibility requires that human persons choose between multiple legitimate options. The idea of alternate possibilities seems to lie at the core of the notion of "choice" so important to discussions of free will. Yet, as we have seen, the truth of determinism entails the denial that there are multiple legitimate possibilities given any particular set of circumstances. Instead, of a series of forking paths, you have a single straight line extending into the future. On this argument, however, if determinism entails the denial of alternative possibilities, it must also entail the denial of free will and responsibility.

Consequently, some compatibilists attack the premise that alternate possibilities are necessary for affirming moral responsibility. Harry Frankfurt has famously used a number of thought experiments to support his argument. In one example, Frankfurt calls on us to imagine that someone, call him Black, wants to make sure that another person, Jones, performs a certain action, A. Suppose further that he has developed the means to monitor Jones' internal states to determine what action he was about to perform and some means for making Jones do whatever Black wants (e.g., a neural implant or drugs). He would prefer that Jones perform the action on his own, but he is willing to intervene and make Jones choose A if he determines that Jones is about to choose B instead. Now suppose that Jones chooses A on his own and that Black does not intervene. According to Frankfurt, Jones has no alternate possibilities in this scenario; he must do A. Yet we would still view this as a responsible action because he freely chose A. Thus, alternate possibilities are not necessary for responsibility.

One common objection to Frankfurt-style arguments is that Jones actually did have alternate possibilities, but they preceded his decision for A. For Black to monitor Jones and determine what Jones was about to do, there must have been something that Jones did before A, call it A_0, that indicated what his choice was going to be. So, Jones had a choice between A_0 and B_0 and Black only intervenes when he determines that Jones has decided on B_0. To eliminate this alternate possibility, Black would need to intervene at this earlier stage and make sure that Jones chose A_0. But this, of course, only pushes the problem back one step and the compatibilist runs into a regress problem.

The compatibilist has two ways of addressing this. First, he can extend Black's involvement with Jones to encompass Jones's entire life. Suppose that Black exercises a kind of global control over Jones, but that Jones always acts in the way that Black wants. Jones thus acts freely throughout his life, because Black never intervened, but never has any real alternate possibilities because Black was always poised to step in and make Jones act in different ways if necessary.

Even on this scenario, however, it seems that Jones has legitimate alternative possibilities because it is always possible that he will begin to choose differently than Black wants (or, that he will do whatever he must do prior to making a choice that would signal to Black that he was about to make such a choice) and cause Black to intervene.

Second, the compatibilist can deny that A_0 is a voluntary event. If we suppose instead that A_0 is the involuntary consequence of some prior causal process, then there is no difficulty with Black monitoring that causal process to determine if its outcome will be A_0 or B_0, and intervening on that basis. Whether one finds this argument convincing, however, depends almost entirely on whether one thinks that a choice that is produced entirely by a deterministic and involuntary process can still be considered a responsible action. Libertarians will argue that the kind of determinism involved in this scenario removes Jones's responsibility because he is neither the source of this action nor in control. So, they contend that this kind of Frankfurt-style argument only succeeds in blocking alternate possibilities by removing responsibility.

Even if Frankfurt-style arguments were successful in establishing that alternate possibilities were unnecessary for grounding moral responsibility, however, it is not clear that this would make for a more satisfying understanding of free will. Removing alternate possibilities alone is insufficient for addressing the problems of *ownership* and *control* that plague classic compatibilism. In other words, as Timothy O'Connor argues, the key issue is not whether I have alternate possibilities, but whether I can be viewed as the primary agent who is the owner and originator of my own actions.[14] Thus, the libertarian could possibly concede that alternate possibilities are not necessary for moral responsibility and still deny the legitimacy of compatibilism.

The ownership argument. Another set of concerns leveled against compatibilism has do to with its account of how "willing" is grounded in the human agent. Many question whether compatibilism provides an adequate explanation of how my decisions are really *mine*. This argument can be presented roughly as follows:

1. A person acts freely only if she is the ultimate source of that action.
2. Determinism entails that no person is the ultimate source of her action.
3. Therefore, determinism entails that no person acts freely.

This concern is driven primarily by the concern that if all of my actions, including my free decisions, are ultimately determined by and grounded in antecedent causal factors that are external to me, then it becomes difficult to understand how they can be viewed as *my* actions and decisions. Should we not rather say that they "belong" to the causal factors that produced them? Although I am certainly involved in their production, it would seem that I am merely another link in the causal chain and that there is no reason to identify the result with my particular link more than any of the others.

Classic compatibilism in particular has a difficult time with this argument since, as we have seen, it focuses exclusively on the person's desires irrespective of the source of those desires. Newer forms of compatibilism, however, struggle with this argument as well. The hierarchicalist contends that actions are properly owned by human persons when they cohere with their higher-order desires or deepest selves. Yet do we really want to deny that the person acts freely when they act contrary their highest values? There may be some value in seeing this as less than truly free insofar as it does not express my deepest convictions and values; nevertheless, we should still place it within the broader category of free and responsible volitions.

Another problem arises when we consider the possibility of conflicting higher-order desires. Human persons are often ambivalent about their actions. Suppose that I want to be truthful with my wife and preserve fidelity within the relationship, but I also want some benefit that will come about as a result of lying. Thus, I have a second-order desire to want to give into the compulsion and lie to my wife and *at the same time* I have a second-order desire not to want to do this. This situation would seem to require that I reflect on my second-order desires based on a third-order desire (i.e., a desire about which second-order desire I want to have), and a regress looms again. To prevent this, Frankfurt argues that we do not reflect indefinitely on our higher-order desires, but that at some point we simply *identify* with one desire rather than the other as most true of who we want to be. To prevent this from sounding entirely arbitrary, Frankfurt contends that the higher-order desires that we eventually identify with are those that we can *wholeheartedly* identify with because they are the ones that we ultimately find most satisfying. As several critics have pointed out, however, the very notion of wholehearted identification is itself a volitional concept that raises all the problems of control, source, and alternate possibilities all over again.

Finally, suppose that B. F. Skinner succeeded in conditioning a group of people to have a particular set of deepest desires and always to act consistently with those deepest desires. This would seem to constitute a free action for the hierarchicalist even though it would also seem that such pervasive conditioning precludes the possibility of free action. One could address this problem by arguing that control over higher-order desires is unnecessary for grounding moral responsibility. Instead, I need only *endorse* them. That is, as long as I affirm that these desires are mine, it does not matter where they came from. This could be strengthened further by maintaining that my action is free as long as I endorse the higher-order desires, and that I would continue to do so even if I knew the set of conditions that produced it. However, suppose that Skinner also conditioned his test subjects such that they would endorse the actions as truly theirs even if they were fully informed about the reality of their conditioning.[15] It would seem, then, that no matter what the hierarchicalist does, it remains difficult to understand how actions that are ultimately sourced outside the human agent can fully be said to belong to that agent in ways that do not undermine responsibility.

The reasons-responsiveness approach offers a slightly different response to this objection but struggles with difficulties of its own. The model outlined above will not work against a reasons-response portrayal of compatibilism, because that kind of conditioning would make those individuals nonresponsive to rational considerations. Yet the model could be adjusted slightly to account for this. Instead of simply conditioning the test subjects to desire certain things and act accordingly, Skinner could condition his subjects to find certain reasons more compelling than others. Thus, the test subjects remain reasons-responsive in that they would act different if they found an alternative set of reasons more compelling, but their actions are fully determined in that Skinner has established precisely which set of reasons they will actually find compelling.

Although these manipulation arguments may seem far-fetched, they do indicate that the main options available to contemporary compatibilists' all struggle to explain how an agent's willings are sufficiently grounded in the agent to qualify as his or her own. Manipulation arguments point out that insofar as the decisions and actions are ultimately sourced outside the human agent, it is difficult to identify them with that agent in ways that do not undermine responsibility.

The problem of evil argument. Although we cannot go into an extended discussion of the problem of evil here, no discussion of free will would be complete without some comment on this issue. For many theologians, the existence of sin and evil in the world constitutes one of the most decisive objections to compatibilism. Where do sin and evil come from? If God is completely in control of everything, including the desires, character, and other factors that determine human free actions, it would seem that God is responsible for all of the sin and evil that occur in the world. If we deny that he is the author of sin, it would seem that we must reject the compatibilist contention that he is the ultimate cause of everything that happens.

Compatibilists have traditionally offered a number of responses to this problem. First, some contend that God does not actually *cause* sinful action, he simply *permits* them.[16] Thus, he does not actually produce the action, although he could have prevented it had he chosen to do so. Given the theistic compatibilist contention that free human actions are divinely determined, however, a merely passive understanding of God's permissive will does not suffice. It is not the case that some human actions are produced autonomously and that God may choose whether to intervene; rather, for the compatibilist, God determines all human actions. In a compatibilist's system, then, although one might use "permission" language to distinguish between different ways in which God wills free actions, such language cannot denote a difference between actions in which God is casually active and those in which he is not.

Another approach contends that God is not responsible for sinful actions because the human agent performs such actions willingly and in complete accord with his or her own desires. Thus, John Feinberg argues, "When we sin, God neither does the act nor enables it (as with righteous deeds) by doing it through the sinner. He doesn't need to do any of this, for we are thoroughly able and willing to do it on our own. So God is neither the proximate cause nor the remote cause of such acts in the sense of being the ultimate mover of the act."[17] Yet this approach seems to ignore that for the compatibilist, God is the ultimate source of the very desires that produced the action (or, at least, he is the ultimate cause of the causal chain that produced those desires). Thus, even if we hold that I am also responsible for the action, it is not clear why this would absolve God from the responsibility that would seem to accrue to himself as the one ultimately responsible for the production of the action.

Some compatibilists will simply bite the bullet and acknowledge that their system does entail God's responsibility for sin and evil. However, they often maintain that this is not theologically problematic because God's actions are done with respect to a higher purpose. Thus, for example, Leibniz famously argued that this is the "best of all possible worlds" and Jonathan Edwards contended that even sin and evil are simply the means by which God accomplishes the higher end of manifesting his own glory.[18] Few are satisfied, however, with the marginalization of sin and evil that such an approach entails.

A last response offered by many compatibilists is to point out that divine responsibility for sin and evil is a problem for all orthodox theologies and not compatibilism alone. All orthodox theologies maintain that God created everything with complete foreknowledge of what would result and that he had the power and ability either to refrain from creating or to intervene so as to prevent sin and evil from happening. Any such account of God must explain why God should not be held responsible (or, why it should not e a problem even if we do view him as responsible) for whatever happens as a result of his creation and providential sustenance of the world.[19]

Libertarianism

An entirely different approach is taken by those who reject the compatibility of determinism and free will. In its simplest form, libertarianism maintains something like the following:

1. determinism and free will are incompatible;
2. free will exists; therefore
3. determinism is false.[20]

Libertarians thus agree with the hard determinists that free will and determinism are ultimately incompatible. Unlike the hard determinists, however, libertarians are convinced that "free will" is a basic datum of human experience and cannot be rejected. Consequently, libertarians take the opposite approach and deny the truth of determinism.

For libertarians, the incompatibility of free will and determinism is established once we realize that true free will requires that human persons be the ultimate source of their actions in such a way that they exercise meaningful control in choosing between various, legitimate alternatives. Thus, for the libertarian, issues of source, control, and alternative possibilities suffice to establish that free will and determinism are simply incompatible.

Indeed, many find this kind of freedom throughout the Bible. Thus, we have biblical texts declaring that people must choose whether they will follow God (e.g., Deut. 30.15–19; Josh. 24.15; Jer. 7.1–15; Jn. 3.16–18), and others in which God commands people to make certain choices with the expectation that they are able to respond (e.g., Ezek. 14.6; Mt. 3.2) and holding them accountable for their actions (e.g., Ezek. 24.14; Rom. 2.5–6). For the libertarian, such commands and expectations make sense only if we presume that human persons exercise sufficient control over their actions such that they are able to make alternative choices and, consequently, can be held responsible for the choices that they do make. In addition, as we have seen, many are convinced that some form of libertarian freedom is necessary to resolve the tensions created by the problems of sin and evil. Thus, people find biblical and theological as well as philosophical reasons for affirming the truth of libertarianism.

Libertarians, however, are faced with their own set of problems. Most important, many are convinced that the libertarian understanding of free will ultimately founders on concerns regarding whether indeterminism of any kind implies a kind of randomness and arbitrariness that ultimately undermines responsibility. As Polanyi declared, "Responsible action excludes randomness."[21] Thus, like compatibilism, many reject libertarianism because they find it inadequate to ground moral responsibility.

The various types of libertarianism can be differentiated primarily by how they understand causation with respect to free actions.

Non-causal libertarianism. As we will see shortly, the libertarian runs into a number of problems as soon as he allows that free decisions are caused in some way. What is the cause? What caused the cause? How is the cause related to the free act? And how do we develop a causal account that rejects determinism without lapsing into some form of randomness or overt appeal to mystery? Such concerns have led some to believe that we should reject the notion that free actions are *caused* at all.[22] Instead, volitions are basic mental events that have no intrinsic causal structure. That is, they simply *are*; they are not caused by anything more basic. In this way, volitions stand outside the causal chains that govern physical events.

If free actions are not caused, however, one immediately begins to wonder how such actions are related to the reasons and desires that I have for acting. On the noncausal account, volitions are connected to actions through the "intentional" content of the action. That is, the content of my volitional decision to watch *Pirates of the Caribbean* comprises my desire to do so and the reasons I have for thinking that this action will satisfy my desires. This volition does not cause me to watch the movie. Instead, the volition is related to its effect in one of two ways. On one account, the intention is related to the action just in case it seems to the agent as though he or she were producing the action as a result of the intention. A second approach contends that the action is properly related to the agent just in case the agent acts in a way that is in accord with his or her intentions. Thus, we can say that my decision to watch *Pirates of the Caribbean* is appropriately related to my action just in case (1) it seems to me that they are so related or (2) there is concord between my action and the intentional content of my volition.

Either account, however, promotes a connection between the volition and action that is tenuous at best. Neither approach has any obvious way of establishing whether there is a real connection between the volition and the action beyond the subjective experience of the agent or their circumstantial correspondence in the agent's action. On both accounts, it remains entirely possible that some other agent is actually the one bringing about the action. If this is the case, however, the noncausal account seems unable to establish that the action is reasons-responsive and under the control of the agent. As we have seen, without these it is hard to see how one could develop a meaningful account of free will. Thus, most libertarians opt for one of the other two approaches we will consider.

Event-causal libertarianism. Most libertarians affirm that free volitions are caused in some way but that they remain undetermined. On this view, the agent is faced with a choice between E and F, and there are no antecedent circumstances sufficient for determining which he will choose. Certainly the agent's beliefs/desires/character will incline him (sometimes strongly) in one direction or another, but they do not absolutely determine which of the two he will choose. For the reasons discussed above, these thinkers find it entirely unconvincing to argue that the free volition is uncaused. So, something must tip the scales and make the agent choose E rather than F. But what is it?

One approach appeals to the concept of "event-causation" to explain how this happens. Event-causation maintains that everything that happens in the world is caused by some antecedent event. Thus, a proper causal account involves an event that produces some corresponding result (which can, in turn, serve as the cause of some subsequent event). We can, of course, trace the causal chain further by referencing even earlier events. This event-causal understanding of human action is most commonly found in deterministic approaches to free will. The human person stands in the causal chain of events and, consequently, his or her actions are entirely determined. The event-causal libertarian, then, must provide some way of understanding event-causation that avoids this deterministic conclusion. The most prominent such approach has been developed by Robert Kane. According to Kane, for an action to be free, it must be one for which the agent is "ultimately responsible." As Kane argues, "to be *ultimately responsible* for an action, an agent must be responsible for anything that is a sufficient reason, cause, or motive for the action's occurring."[23]

This immediately raises the question, however, of whether Kane's position generates an infinite regress. In order for me to be responsible for C, I have to be responsible for the event B that produced C. Of course, I must then be responsible as well for A, and the regress looms. Kane recognizes the problem, however, and contends that the regress can be stopped by positing that on some occasions an agent faces a choice between two possibilities in which the agent's will is not already settled and that on those occasions the agent makes an effort of the will to settle on one option and that the agent's choice and its corresponding action forms the agent's will in a way that will then guide subsequent choices. Such "will setting" actions, then, are basic to the way in which an agent is formed to be the kind of agent that he or she is—they are "self-forming actions."

Such self-forming actions, for Kane, must meet three conditions— they must be done *voluntarily* (willingly), *intentionally* (knowingly), and *rationally* (having good reasons for acting in this way). Furthermore, because will-setting actions are necessarily open to more than one option (i.e., they are not already will-settled), they must be voluntary, intentional, and rational "*whichever* way they go."[24]

Agent-causal libertarianism. In the next section we will consider a number of arguments that raise some real questions about the viability of event-causal libertarianism. Some libertarians contend, then, that we should reject the idea that free actions are caused by antecedent events. Instead, we should simply recognize that the cause of a person's free actions is the person himself or herself. Thus, although agent causalists typically affirm event-causal accounts of most events, they deny that event-causation is sufficient to capture the essence of free human actions. Instead, they contend that human persons are capable of causing an action directly—that is, not by virtue of doing something else or existing in some state of affairs. They typically posit that there is a *primitive* or *brute* causal relation between an agent and its body that cannot be broken down into more basic causal relations.

According to Robert Chisholm, one well-known proponent of this idea, some form of agent causation is necessary to avoid a regress that would fatally undermine agential responsibility. For example, with respect to a man's hand moving a staff, he argues,

> We *may* say that the hand was moved by the man, but we may *also* say that the motion of the hand was caused by the motion of certain muscles; and we may say that the motion of the muscles was caused by certain events that took place within the brain. But some event, and presumably one of those that took place within the brain, was caused by the agent and not by any other events.[25]

In other words, if we do not stop the regress of casual events at some point, we will lose the ability to say that the man himself actually *did* anything meaningful.

The agent-causalist, then, avoids the problem of determinism by appealing to some *thing* (agent, mind, soul, etc.) that lies outside the determinist causal framework. Although most events (physical, spiritual, etc.) may be deterministically produced by antecedent circumstances (the agent-causalist can actually remain agnostic on whether this is the case), the agent himself or herself is simply not a part of this causal framework.

Arguments against libertarianism
The luck argument. One of the most commonly cited arguments against libertarian views of free will is that their emphasis on the indeterminate nature of free actions renders those actions purely the result of luck. To see this, consider my decision D. According to the classic libertarian position, if D is a free choice, it must be undetermined. That means that a different choice must have been possible for me *given exactly the same set of antecedent conditions.*

In other words, if we rewound the tape of my life to just before I decided *D* and played the scenario again with exactly the same external circumstances and internal conditions (reasons, desires, values, etc.), it is entirely possible that I would choose *E* this time around. If this is the case, however, it would seem that the decision was not actually under my control and that it was merely a matter of chance that I chose *D* rather than *E*. An action that comes about as a result of mere chance, however, can hardly be an action for I should be held responsible.

This problem arises most clearly in any attempt to appeal to quantum indeterminateness as an explanation for how free will might exist in the universe. According to this argument, quantum physics entails that our universe is characterized at its most fundamental level by random indeterminism.[26] The existence of such pervasive indeterminateness might seem to give us a way of explaining how a mental event (e.g., a volition) could occur without being determinately caused by some antecedent sufficient cause. However, notice that this does not really provide us with the kind of controlled and properly sourced action the libertarian is looking for. Instead of being the free volition of a meaningfully responsible agent, the choice is now presented as a mere happenstance. Why did I choose *D*? Random quantum fluctuations in my brain just happened to settle on *D*. How could I be held responsible for an action that is the result of a purely random process? Indeed, it is difficult to see how I could be called the agent of such an action at all. Rather than being a morally responsible agent, I seem to a bystander waiting to see what random action I will be performing next. Any appeal to indeterminism, then, seems to undermine the ability of libertarianism to ground agency and moral responsibility.

Libertarians have a number of ways to respond to this argument. Noncausal libertarians, of course, simply deny that the volition is caused at all, indeterministically or otherwise. This is only accomplished, however, by unacceptably severing the connection between the volition and the event. Other libertarians must offer a way of understanding the causal connection that allows for some level of indeterminism but without falling pretty to the luck problem.

One common approach is to point out that indeterminism does not entail that all of the options are *equally* possible. The external and internal conditions of my action may make me decidedly more inclined toward *D* than *E*. Thus, Timothy O'Connor is right to point out that libertarianism does not portray the human person as an "unmoved mover" but rather as a "not wholly moved mover." Yet for the classic libertarian, it must be the case that both D and E were fully possible for my action to be free. Thus, even if D were more probable than E, until I actually made my choice, it was undetermined which choice I would make. Making one of the two more probable, then, does not erase the difficulties raised by the luck argument.

Another approach offered by Robert Kane is that the agent makes an effort of will toward only one of the available choices but that it is indeterministically open whether this effort will succeed. Thus, I make an effort of the will to choose to tell my wife the truth, but it is entirely possible that this effort will fail and that I will lie to my wife instead. There are at least two key problems with this approach, however. First, this construal dodges the question of how I came to make this particular effort of the will and not the other. As with many of the positions we've considered, this approach seems simply to push the problem back one step. Second, it is not clear on this account how I can be held responsible for those actions that resulted from a failed effort of the will. Surely, I can be held responsible for attempting to form a volition to tell my wife the truth, but how can I be similarly responsible for the indeterministic, and apparently random, failure of that effort?

Kane's more recent arguments try to resolve the luck objection by arguing that in "self-forming actions," the agent actually makes an effort of will in both directions (i.e., I make an effort of will both to choose to tell my wife the truth *and* to choose to lie to her), but it is indeterministically open which of the two will succeed. Regardless, as both will-efforts are done voluntarily, intentionally, and rationally, they are still actions for which I am ultimately responsible and morally accountable. This argument, however, also fails to satisfy. At the very least, it renders the action morally ambiguous because I would seem to be both morally blameworthy and praiseworthy at the same time, even when the resulting action itself was praiseworthy. The corresponding complexity of requiring duplicate willings for every self-forming action also raises questions about the adequacy of the approach.

A more adequate response to the luck argument needs to offer an account of how the agent's reasons, beliefs, and character are causally significant in the production of the free action while still retaining the idea that the free action was undetermined. The possibility of developing such a libertarian account leads us into the next argument.

The Reasons-response argument. Somewhat akin to the luck argument, this argument contends that the indeterministic nature of libertarianism means that free actions are not reasons-responsive and, consequently, are arbitrary and irrational. Thus, as Bruce Ware contends, "More simply, no choice-specific reason or reasons can be given for any so-called free choices or actions that we do. Of course, this reduces all 'free' choices and actions to arbitrariness and removes from us the bases for why we choose and act."[27] The libertarian, then, must find a way of affirming out the person's actions, *a*, are properly related and responsive to the person's reasons, *r*.

This constitutes a decisive problem for noncausal accounts. Regardless of which form of noncausal libertarianism is in view, the tenuousness of the connection between *a* and *r* renders it possible that something else entirely is what actually causes an agent to act in the way that he or she does. An event-causal account, on the other hand, struggles to find a way of affirming the reasons-responsiveness of free actions without lapsing into determinism or irrationality. For event-causal libertarianism to work, there must be some level of indeterminism in the free action. But where does the event-causalist locate the indeterminism? If he places the indeterminism between *r* and *a*—or, in contrast, within *r* itself—then the action becomes random and arbitrary. Another option would be to place the indeterminism before *r*. On such an account, the thoughts and ideas that come to mind as objects of deliberation are indeterministically produced, but once they come to mind, the deliberation process and the consequent action are entirely deterministic.[28] Thus, the entire sequence is undetermined, as it was undetermined which thoughts and ideas would factor into the deliberation, but the action remains reasons-responsive throughout. Such an account, however, seems to rob the person of any significant involvement in the production of his or her own actions. To see this, suppose that we invented a machine that would perform three actions depending on which of three buttons was pushed. Then suppose that we created an indeterministic process that would lead to one of the three buttons being pushed. In such a scenario, the eventual outcome is undetermined, but this would not make it the case that the machine was responsible for the action. So, it would seem that an event-causal account struggles to find a place to locate indeterminism in the rational production of an action without lapsing into arbitrariness.

Agent-causalists likewise try to offer an account of reasons-responsiveness. Indeed, as Timothy O'Connor contends, "The viability of the agency theorist's framework for understanding free will crucially depends on its capacity to leave these [reason] explanations largely intact."[29] O'Connor thus argues that although reasons do not cause free actions, because libertarianly free actions are always undetermined, they are, nevertheless, causally significant in that they form the context within which decisions are made.

> I don't introduce events ex nihilo; (at best) I influence the direction of what is already there. What is there is a structured, dynamic situation open to some possibilities and not to others, and the nested structure of conative and cognitive factors that I refer to as "my reasons" is among the most basic factors that circumscribe my capacity to exercise a limited degree of autonomy. (Active power is the power to freely choose one's course for reasons.)[30]

Thus, the agent's reasons, desires, and character are causally significant in that they provide the context within which the agent chooses to act. The agent remains the sole cause of the action, although she does so under the influence of these causally significant factors. Thus, agents "cause intentions in virtue of reasons."[31] Free actions can be rational and explicable because they provide the context within which an agent chooses and acts. The action remains undetermined, however, in that the agent is free to decide differently. It remains possible that in any given situation, the agent could weigh these various factors differently and draw a different conclusion.[32]

Of all the explanations offered, the agent-causal account seems to provide the most helpful account of how reasons factor into the agent's decisions and actions. The agent-causal solution, however, contributes to another problem.

The mystery argument. The primary criticism of the agent-causal approach to free will is that it posits a causal relation between the agent and his or her volitions that is fundamentally mysterious. As Lynne Rudder-Baker complains, "they simply postulate a power that meets libertarian conditions for free will without making plausible how we could have such an amazing power."[33] By appealing to a unique kind of brute causal relation, the agent-causalist may succeed in avoiding determinism, but only at the cost of appealing to a fundamental mystery. As many critics point out, agent-causation seems simply to identify what is necessary to ground its indeterminist framework and then define it into existence.

The agent-causalist typically responds to this objection by arguing that it misses the point. As agent-causation is fundamentally different than other kinds of causation, they contend that it is a mistake to ask for an explanation of the causal relation. Indeed, given the agent-causal contention that the causal relation is brute, there cannot be a more fundamental causal explanation. Agents are not events that need to be caused by prior events. This response, however, amounts to an appeal to the basic mysteriousness of agent-causation that drives the criticism. For many critics, the fact that agent-causation has to appeal to mystery as a solution demonstrates its inherent weakness (and maybe incoherence).

Along the same lines, some wonder whether agent-causation really provides a framework for understanding the action as under the control of the agent. As the causal relation is brute and inexplicable, we really have no way of establishing that the agent himself or herself is actually in control of the action. Although the agent-causalist can stipulate that agent-causation is by definition under the control of the agent, by doing so he or she once again demonstrates that agent-causation can only answer objections by fiat.

The foreknowledge argument. The most prominent theological problem associated with libertarianism is that of divine foreknowledge. Actually, there are two problems here. The first problem, that of showing how foreknowledge and free will can be compatible, can be summarized as follows. God's infallible foreknowledge entails that yesterday God infallibly knew that I would choose D today. As this knowledge is infallible, this would mean that yesterday it was true that I would choose D today. If this was true yesterday, however, it would also be true today that I would choose D. Thus, it would seem that given God's infallible foreknowledge of today's events, there is only one possible outcome in this situation—I will choose D. I do not seem to have alternate possibilities in this situation and, consequently, I am not libertarianly free. Thus, infallible divine foreknowledge and libertarian freedom, on this rendering, are incompatible. The second problem takes a slightly different form. Unlike compatibilistically free actions, libertarianly free actions cannot be predicted based on the their antecedent circumstances. Instead, libertarianly

free decisions remain unpredictable (beyond mere probabilistic pre-
diction) up to the moment of decision. If this is the case, however,
how can it be that God, or anyone, could infallibly know what decision would be made? Both arguments, then, suggest that infallible
divine foreknowledge and libertarian free will are incompatible.

Libertarians have offered quite a number of different responses to
this old argument. We will consider a few of the more prominent
solutions. First, theologians have long contended that the mistake in
the argument begins with the suggestion that God knew something
"yesterday." Theologians inclined to view God as transcending temporal realities (i.e., divine timelessness) contend that God does not
know or experience events in sequence as we do; rather, he experiences temporal events in one eternal "now." Thus, there are multiple
legitimate options in any libertarianly free situation *at the same time
that* God infallibly knows what decision will be produced because
God transcends the temporal linearity that causes the problem.
Although this might address the problem of foreknowledge, however, many thinkers are opposed to this way of understanding God's
relationship to time for other reasons.[34]

An alternative solution appeals to God's "middle knowledge" of
contingent events. This approach, *molinism*, argues that God has
three different kinds of knowledge. He has knowledge of necessary
truths and of those things that he will bring about through his own
creative will. In addition, he also has "middle" knowledge of what a
free creature *would do* in any specific set of circumstances. Thus, what
God foreknows are the "counterfactuals" of freedom. From this
perspective, the person can be libertarianly free in a given situation in
which he or she is faced with multiple real possibilities, but that God
has infallibly true knowledge of the counterfactual truths of what
the person will do in that situation. Molinism has been subjected to
a number of important critiques.[35] Most importantly, many contend
that these "counterfactuals" are not real objects of knowledge and,
consequently, can provide no basis for God's knowledge of future
free actions. Others have argued that even if Molinism is coherent, it
provides no real help in responding to the foreknowledge argument.
Given God's middle knowledge of counterfactuals, it remains the case
that in any actual circumstance in which I find myself, there is only
possible outcome. Of course, there *could have been* other outcomes had
the circumstances been different, but this runs into the same difficulties of hypothetical conditionality we encountered in compatibilism.

A final option is to reject one of the premises of the argument. One could either deny that God has infallible divine foreknowledge of future free events, or one could deny that a lack of alternative possibilities necessarily undermines libertarian free will. The first path is taken by "open theism." According to this position, God only knows infallibly those things that can be known. Since future free events do not yet exist, they do not qualify as things that "can be known." Consequently, God does not know them. While this approach has received significant attention in recent years, it has not garnered much support. A second option would be to contend that alternative possibilities are not really necessary for libertarianism. We have already seen that some libertarians are willing to acknowledge that alternative possibilities might not be necessary to ground moral responsibility. Maybe a similar solution would suffice here. Thus, a libertarian opting for this solution could argue that all that is necessary for libertarian free will is that the agent be the "ultimate source" or her volitions. Although God infallibly foreknows what will choice will be made in any particular instance, it remains the case that nothing external to the agent causes the agent to make any particular choice. On this account, then, control and ownership are sufficient to ground libertarian freedom.

We can thus see that libertarians have a number of options available to them for responding to the problem of foreknowledge. How successful each is depends largely on whether we are willing to live with some of corresponding weaknesses. It seems to me that the likeliest candidates for a successful libertarian response to the argument lie either in the appeal to God's timelessness or the denial that libertarianism requires alternative possibilities. Either of these approaches provides the libertarian with adequate ways forward.

THE STATE OF THE DEBATE

Despite millennia of dialogue, the free will debate continues without resolution. From one perspective it might seem that compatibilism has largely won the day. Thus, Daniel Dennett notes that compatibilism is "the unargued ambient worldview of the scientific community" today.[36] Compatibilism is likewise affirmed by a substantial number of contemporary philosophers and theologians. Nonetheless, libertarianism retains strong support among all three groups. Even though a majority of contemporary philosophers continue to argue for some form of compatibilism, the opposite is true among philosophers working specifically on the problem of free will.[37] Among scientists, the rise of indeterminist interpretations of quantum physics has contributed to a growing move away from determinist ways of understanding human nature. Add to this the fact that most theologians espouse some form of libertarianism and its widespread assumption at the popular level, and the picture shifts from a prevailing compatibilism to a much more prominent libertarian perspective. Either way, the debate is far from over. Given the fundamental differences that divide the two camps as well as the length and complexity of the debate, it seems unlikely that a resolution will be forthcoming any time soon.

A WAY FORWARD: FRAMING THE DEBATE

Once again, then, we have encountered a seemingly irresoluble anthropological debate. Each side has powerful arguments, yet each side also manifests significant weaknesses. Once again, there does not appear to be any easy way of resolving the problem through direct appeal to the biblical texts. Thinkers from both perspectives cite a whole range of biblical texts in support of their position, with each offering ways of understanding apparently contrary texts in ways consistent with their position. Once again, then, we find ourselves addressing a debate that has a direct bearing on important biblical concepts but with regard to which the Bible does not seem to offer a specific answer. Thus, as John Feinberg contends, "Scripture does not say what sort of freedom we have; it only teaches that we are free"; consequently, "we cannot prove either libertarian or compatibilistic free will just by citing passages that teach human freedom and/or moral responsibility."[38]

The free will debate is seriously complicated by the fact that successful resolution of the debates requires the various parties to have clear and agreed upon definitions of two basic concepts, and there is little clarity about either of them. First, most of our previous discussion has assumed that we know what it means for an action/event/person to "cause" something. Yet causation is a notoriously difficult concept to define, and there is little agreement in philosophy or science about what qualifies as a cause or exactly what relates a cause to its effect.[39] The situation is further complicated by the fact that most of us continue to operate with a rather Newtonian understanding of the universe in which causes produce effects in a deterministic and linear fashion. Thus, proponents of each approach argue about how to relate deterministic physical causes to the apparently "free" actions of human persons. Contemporary developments in quantum physics, chaos theory, and other disciplines present an entirely different understanding of the universe, one in which causal relations are far more difficult to trace. Without an agreed upon basis for discussing the nature of causation, however, it is not at all clear how the free will debate can proceed. How can the libertarians continue to critique compatibilism for holding to an unacceptable form of determinism without offering a definition of causation that explains what determinism even means in such a context? And how can compatibilists continue to critique libertarianism for entailing that undetermined actions are inherently random and arbitrary without offering a definition of causation that explains why such must be the case? Advocates on both sides need to do more work understanding and explaining their intuitions regarding causation and what exactly generates the relevant problems for their opponents.

A second issue is equally as challenging. Advocates on both sides of the debate argue that we must affirm that human persons are morally responsible beings. Indeed, the debate is often framed specifically as a debate about what view of free will is adequate to ground moral responsibility. Yet there is little consensus as to precisely what constitutes "responsibility" itself. Thus, proponents of each perspective criticize their counterparts for failing to uphold a version of free will that is compatible with responsibility. Yet neither side is able to present a convincing account of exactly what is necessary for a human person to be held responsible for her actions. Lacking such an account, the free will argument often lapses into a conflict of intuitions regarding what suffices for human responsibility. Thus, David Ciocchi calls for an "agnostic autonomism" that affirms whatever kind of free will is necessary to ground human responsibility while recognizing its current inability to explain precisely what kind of free will that might be.[40]

Lacking clarity on these two points, an adequate resolution to the free will debate seems unlikely. Nonetheless, we can weigh the relative strengths and weaknesses of the various positions by considering the extent to which they are able to affirm coherently the key tenets of our theological anthropology.

A number of these theories explicitly affirm that there is some-thing about the human person as a free being that transcends easy answers and defies reductionistic analysis. Thus, many of these think-ers begin their discussions by affirming a significant level of *mystery* at the core of the debate. We must always be careful, however, about appealing to mystery too quickly as a resolution to philosophical and theological dilemmas. Such appeals to mystery can in fact serve to truncate valuable discussion and the benefit that accrues from wrestling through demanding problems. Nonetheless, as we have seen, causation itself can be understood as fundamentally mysteri-ous, and the mystery only deepens when one tries to understand the relationship between human and divine causality. So, until more clarity is achieved, if it ever is, about the nature of causality, the rela-tionship between various causes, and the kind of cause/effect rela-tionship necessary to ground moral responsibility, we will to continue affirming that there is something transcendentally mysterious about the free actions of human persons in the world.

Likewise, both approaches affirm the *relative uniqueness* of the human person. Each recognizes that many of the capacities humans use when they make free choices are shared to at least some extent with other animals. Thus, many animals, particularly the other higher primates, exercise various levels of rationality, weigh consequences, and choose among competing alternatives. At the same time, each recognizes some level of uniqueness regarding human volitionality. Typically, humans alone are viewed as acting with the kind of free will necessary for moral responsibility. We can train animals to behave properly, but we rarely see them as morally culpable for their actions (unless we are particularly frustrated with them). The two approaches, of course, differ in how they nuance this relative uniqueness. Com-patibilists (particularly those of a more physicalist bent) will often be more inclined to emphasize that which humans have in common with other animals, whereas libertarians (particularly agent-causal libertarians) will focus more on that which makes humans unique in creation. Nonetheless, there does not seem to be any reason to suppose that either is incapable of affirming this important anthro-pological truth.

Finally, neither has any difficulty with the *brokenness* and *relation-ality* of the human person. Or, at least, neither has any *necessary* difficulty with these affirmations. It is certainly the case, however, that much of the debate (particularly from the libertarian perspective) tends to portray the human person as a relatively autonomous and properly functioning being. Thus, there tends to be little discussion of the role that broader social and cultural relationships play in the volitionality of the individual person, or the impact that sin and evil have on the proper function (or malfunction) of the human will. Each can do a better job on both these points. Nonetheless, both have resources for making these affirmations coherently.

On at least three points, however, some more serious questions can be raised. First, we have seen that all of these theories affirm the *moral responsibility* of the human person, most taking this as their point of departure in the discussion. Yet, we have also seen that the coherence of their approach to moral responsibility also constitutes the greatest challenge to the adequacy of their position. In other words, most of these theories affirm the reality of moral responsibility and argue that the philosophical and theological task is to come up with an understanding of free will sufficient for grounding moral responsibility. Yet the significant objections we have encountered raise the question of whether either of these approaches has succeeded in this task. Lacking a convincing argument on this point, then, we may be best served by recognizing that the commitment to moral responsibility is the more fundamental point here. Lacking this, the biblical portrayal of the human person as a moral agent summoned into covenantal relationship with God, each other, and creation, could not stand. We can certainly continue to press for clearer formulations of free will that are capable of affirming this basic responsibility. Indeed, we must do so. At this time, however, given the lack of compelling arguments on either side, we should recognize that each affirms this basic commitment, while continuing to press for clearer and more coherent explanations.

Another difficulty has to do with the extent to which either of these perspectives can be called legitimately *Christocentric*. Although some have attempted to engage the free will debate by looking to the person and work of Jesus Christ, this remains an underdeveloped approach to the problem. This is particularly surprising because the biblical narratives actually have a lot to say about Jesus as a volitional being. He routinely makes decisions and frequently refers to his "will" in connection with the Father's will. Although the Bible says less about the influence of other volitional factors—like external causes and internal states—it is clear in its affirmation that Jesus was a fully human being who exercised his volitionality in the same way that other humans do and, consequently, existed in the same web of causal influences. We certainly cannot attempt to address all of the factors that would arise in such a discussion. At the very least, each approach would need to consider more seriously how it will understand the relation between the divine will and the human will in the incarnation, the nature of Christ's sinlessness and temptation, and the role of the Spirit in the life and volitionality of Christ. With respect to each of these, we need to ask what this Christological reality reveals about what it means to have a "free will" and how this might help us understand the free will debate. Thus, although neither of these approaches necessarily denies the Christocentric reality of the human person, they both have much work to do in this area.

Similarly, although neither approach has any necessary problem affirming *embodiment*, certain libertarian formulations are more problematic than others. For example, although most libertarians fully affirm that human persons are psychophysical beings and that the body is importantly involved in all human actions, the rhetoric often suggests an instrumentalized view of the body that undermines this conviction. The libertarian often paints the picture of the human person acting *through* or *by means of* the body. However, this picture will not do. As we have discussed, the body is not merely the means of the person's action but is intimately involved in the volitional process from beginning to end. The human person (at least in this life) neither wills nor acts independently of his or her body.

CONCLUSION

Working through each of these theories using our criteria for a theologically adequate anthropology, we can see that each struggles at certain key points. Certainly, classic compatibilism is viewed by most as inadequate because of its failure to provide an adequate explanation of where desires and beliefs come from as well as its inadequate explanation of alternate possibilities. New compatibilist theories have worked hard to overcome these weaknesses. Nonetheless, we have seen that they still struggle to explain how the complete determination of the human person's character and affective states does not ultimately undermine the person's responsibility for actions that result from that character and affective condition. The *source* of the person's "deepest self" seems important but unfortunately opaque in the compatibilist system. For theological compatibilists, this leaves them susceptible to concerns surrounding the origin of sin and the nature of evil.

Libertarian theories are subject to important critiques as well. Indeed, the libertarian approach struggles to explain how there can be sufficient indeterminism to allow libertarian free will, without ultimately foundering on the problem of luck or the loss of any causal significance for human reasons, beliefs, and desires. Theologically, libertarianism struggles to explain how God can be causally active in the lives of human persons without undermining their free will.

Our discussion in this chapter has not focused on trying to resolve these debates. Indeed, I have argued that given the currently ambiguous and debated relationship between moral responsibility, causality, and free will, it seems unlikely that the debate will be resolved any time soon. So, as with the mind/body debate, I think that we will be on safer ground identifying those things about the human person that must be affirmed in any adequate theological anthropology and use those as our guiding criteria. With these in place, we can acknowledge that each of these theories has important strengths and corresponding weaknesses. We cannot rule either of them out of bounds on this basis, but we can develop a picture of what any adequate view of free will must be able to affirm and move forward from there.

CHAPTER 6

CONCLUSION

A wonderful fact to reflect upon, that every human creature is constituted to be that profound secret and mystery to every other.
Charles Dickens[1]

OUR HERCULEAN TASK

Unraveling the mystery that is the human person, we begin to feel like Hercules facing his ten tasks. For Hercules, each of these tasks constituted an apparently insurmountable challenge; together, their accomplishment was inconceivable. Similarly, each of the issues that we have addressed in this book constitutes its own set of challenges. Furthermore, each has so frustrated thinkers that they have all been declared to be mysteries in their own right. Thus, each is its own Herculean endeavor. Taken together, the human person appears, not as a singular mystery, but as an intricate interweaving of mysteries that come together in this being who is both a simple member of the animal kingdom and the covenantal co-partner of God, manifesting his personal presence in the world. Unlike Hercules, who had the distinct advantage of being a demigod, we face our task with all the failings and limitations that accompany our finite and fallen human state.

In the face of such a task, we have tried to remain mindful of the fact that we must approach theological anthropology with a firm awareness of the limitations of any anthropological endeavor. Rather than offering definitive solutions to these age-old problems, I have sought to model a particular way of thinking theologically about the human person. This does not mean that we should stop searching for solutions. Indeed, the constant quest for self-knowledge is itself an aspect of what it means to be human, and it certainly functions as an important mechanism for continual self-correction as we bring our concepts of the "true human" under the call to be *semper reformanda*. Thus, the task of theological anthropology is the never-ending process of understanding humanity anew in every age in light of the revelation of humanity given in and through Jesus Christ.

THINKING THEOLOGICALLY ABOUT BEING HUMAN

Throughout these various discussions, my primary concern has been to model a particular way of doing theological anthropology that takes seriously the theological starting point inherent in such a task while also engaging the other anthropological disciplines as legitimate dialogue partners. Thus, theological anthropology takes its seat at the table with a clear understanding that it has a voice in the discussion and that its voice must be heard if humanity is to be understood fully. At the same time, it does not allow its voice to drown out the other participants in the conversation. Instead, it seeks to understand how their insights and contributions might inform and deepen our theological picture of the human; indeed, at times we might even discover that we need to alter our understanding of the theological picture itself. This would happen any time the data produced by the other disciplines caused us to see things in a new way that fostered different ways of readings of the Bible and understanding its portrayal of what it means to be human. This does not place theological anthropology at the mercy of the "sciences," but it does recognize that any theological construction of what it means to be human is itself human and, consequently, subject to the limitations, errors, and abuses of any human endeavor.

With respect to each of the issues in this book, then, I have tried to demonstrate this anthropological method. In the first chapter, I sketched out a basic framework for theological anthropology. The principles developed there are certainly not adequate for a fully developed picture of humanity, but they provided us with a useful starting point for engaging anthropological issues. In each of the three subsequent discussions, I showed how this theological understanding of the human person serves to frame the issue under consideration and assess the various options being proposed. At the same time, we listened carefully to the insights of some of the other disciplines to hear what they might have to say about the problem. Admittedly, our dialog partners have been limited by the scope of this work, and we have interacted mainly with the insights provided by philosophy and psychology, although we have also looked at some of the data produced by biology and the cognitive neurosciences. Nonetheless, the task before us was not to generate a comprehensive understanding of each problem but to consider the basic shape of the problem and see how a theological perspective offers a way forward on each.

IMAGING GOD AS SEXUAL, PSYCHOPHYSICAL, VOLITIONAL BEINGS

We thus began our Herculean task of understanding the human person by asking what it means to affirm that human persons are made "in the image and likeness of God." In doing so, we followed a long-established tradition of viewing the *imago Dei* as a defining concept for theological anthropology, despite the paucity of references outside of the creation narratives. This is so both because of its status as the first theological statement made about the human person and because of the NT's application of the *imago* to the person of Christ and eschatological re-creation of humanity in him. Thus, the *imago* serves both a protological and an eschatological role in understanding the human person. At the same time, we also saw that the *imago* has a continuing function in the present. The *imago* as gift, task, and goal thus encompasses the whole narrative of humanity from beginning to end and can appropriately be used as a central concept of theological anthropology.

What exactly does the *imago Dei* mean? This debated question has produced little unanimity, although several key proposals predominate: the structural, functional, relational, and multifaceted views. Although there are strengths to each of these proposals, I argued that the structural approach is fatally weakened by its lack of exegetical support, the challenge of providing meaningful ways in which humans differ qualitatively from other animals, the inherent difficulty and unfortunate implications of defining humanity in terms of essential structural "capacities" and its overly individualistic and dualistic portrayal of humanity. Similarly, the multifaceted approach, insofar as it relies on aspects of the structural approach, struggles with many of the same problems as well as its own difficulties in explaining how the various facets relate to one another. Having eliminated these two as viable contenders for an adequate under-standing of the *imago Dei*, we focused our attention on the functional and relational concepts. Because each of these enjoys strong support among biblical scholars and theologians, it seemed best to see whether there might be some way of bringing them together in a meaningful synthesis. I argued that this can be done through the idea that human-ity manifests the personal presence of God in the world. In this way, the *imago Dei* is understood both as a function carried out by humans—a task to which human persons have been called—and as an expression of the essential relationality that we see in the triune God and in humans as an interpersonal community.

Finally, having established the best way in which to understand the nature of the *imago Dei*, we also saw how the *imago Dei* can help us develop a theological framework within which to understand the human person. Properly understood, the *imago Dei* creates a way of viewing the human person that emphasizes the centrality of Jesus Christ for understanding human persons, the qualified uniqueness of the human person in creation, the fundamental mystery of humanity, the importance of relationality, responsibility, and embodiment for being truly human, and the necessity of recognizing the brokenness of humanity brought about by the fall into sin. Each of these orients theological anthropology in particular ways and will influence and inform the ways in which we engage all of the other issues that we encounter in the anthropological task.

With this theological framework in place, we moved into a con-sideration of human sexuality, the body/soul relationship, and the nature of free will. With respect to human sexuality, we actually encountered two issues that need to be addressed before we try to deal theologically with questions about gender roles and relation-ships; understanding what gender/sex is and understanding its theological purpose. With respect to the first of these issues, we found that there is more ambiguity in terms such as "male" and "female" than we might have anticipated at first. At the very least we need to recognize the importance of both cultural and biological factors as well as the complex ways in which these two factors interact with and influence each other. On the latter issue, we saw that theologians have approached the question of human sexuality from several different perspectives. Three of those—procreation, fecundity, and marriage—offered helpful perspectives on why sexuality is important for being human, but each did so in ways that that either suggested that sexuality is not really fundamental to being human or implied that certain kinds of people are somehow not fully human. None of these being acceptable, we moved on to consider another approach, namely that of sexuality as the paradigmatic human expression of relationality. Although there is much to be affirmed here, this approach also failed to satisfy in that it again suggested that sexuality is not truly fundamental to being human; it is simply an important expression of that which is truly human. Instead, I argued that human sexuality should be understood from the perspective of "bonding." Our sexuality is fundamentally a drive toward the "other." Thus, rather than being a paradigmatic expression of relationality, sexuality serves as the primary ground of relationality in human persons.

The last two chapters in our study took a slightly different shape. Rather than arguing for a particular perspective on the mind/body and free will questions, I contended that theological anthropology is better served by utilizing its theological framework as a way of orienting the discussion and identifying what is of most vital concern for any adequate theological understanding of the human person. Thus, in the chapter on the mind/body relationship, we surveyed several different ways of viewing human ontology. When placed against the requirements of our theological framework, however, I argued that even though there is much that each perspective can gladly affirm, there are also several points on which they can and should be questioned. Thus, even a properly qualified dualism continues to struggle with explaining, rather than merely affirming, the embodied, psychophysical nature of human life. Physicalism, on the other hand, continues to struggle with its account of personal responsibility, and faces challenging questions on its understanding of consciousness and personal identity. Furthermore, both perspectives find it difficult to talk about mental causation in ways that are both internally coherent and adequate to human experience and the findings of modern science. Thus, rather than offering an argument for either dualism or physicalism, I contended that a properly theological approach to the problem affirms that which is most theologically vital in the discussion, recognizes the weaknesses of all the available theories, and continues to press for more adequate ways of understanding human ontology.

Our discussion of the free will problem took a similar shape as we focused our attention again applying our theological framework to this anthropological problem, rather than attempting to formulate a resolution to this never-ending debate. Thus, we considered the main arguments offered by libertarians and compatibilists and found a number of important strengths and weaknesses with respect to each. Most important, each struggles with significant aspects of how its model for understanding free will affirms the moral responsibility of the human person in a way that coheres with its other fundamental convictions. The compatibilist account raises questions about how we can hold a person responsible for actions that are ultimately sourced outside the human agent herself, whereas the libertarian account struggles with questions of control and responsibility arising from the luck argument and similar criticisms. I also argued that each faces important questions about the adequacy of its understanding of embodiment with respect to free will and the apparent lack of any interest in thinking Christologically about this entire issue.

THE "WHAT" AND THE "WHO" OF HUMANITY

"What is Man?" asks the psalmist. This is a good question. Indeed, it is a necessary question for understanding what it means to be human. Properly understood, however, the primary anthropological question in the Bible is not the "what" question, but the "who" question. "Who" is the human person? On this question the Bible speaks with remarkable clarity. The human person is the one God determined to create in his image and likeness to be the bearers of his presence in the world. The human person is the one with whom God entered into intimate, covenantal relationship, summoning humanity to be his creaturely counterpart and to share in the divine life of the Trinity. The human person is the one who rejected this covenantal relationship, setting off in the autonomous isolation of the *incuravtus* self. The human person is the one who remained the object of God's inconceivable love and unbreakable covenant as he continues the great drama of this divine–human relationship through the history of redemption. Ultimately, however, the human person is the one to whom God appears in unrivalled splendor and humility, mystery and revelation, in the incarnation, drawing humanity ever more closely into the divine life itself. Ultimately, then, we see that the "who" of humanity resides in the "who" of Christology. Who is the human person? The human person is the one called into existence, summoned into partnership, and drawn into relationship in and through Jesus Christ.

Only in light of the "who" question are we in a position to address the "what" question adequately. What is the human person? The human person is, among other things, a being essentially drawn toward relationship with the other, a psychophysical being both grounded in and yet transcendent over its material nature, and a free being capable of engaging in meaningful and accountable relationships. Undoubtedly, we will continue to discuss and debate precisely what we mean when we affirm all of these things about the human person and the particular theories that are most adequate for supporting and sustaining these affirmations. Nonetheless, we have done well if we make these affirmations clearly and confidently in light of the revelation of true humanity found in Christ.

SUGGESTIONS FOR FURTHER READING

General resources in theological anthropology

Anderson, Ray Sherman, *On Being Human: Essays in Theological Anthropology* (Grand Rapids, MI: Eerdmans, 1982).

Berkouwer, G. C., *Man: The Image of God* (Grand Rapids, MI: Eerdmans, 1962).

Jeeves, Malcolm A., *Human Nature: Reflections on the Integration of Psychology and Christianity* (Philadelphia: Templeton Foundation, 2006).

Jewett, Paul K., and Marguerite Shuster, *Who We Are: Our Dignity as Human* (Grand Rapids, MI: Eerdmans, 1996).

McDonald, H. D., *The Christian View of Man* (Westchester, IL: Crossway, 1981).

McFadyen, Alistair, *The Call to Personhood: A Christian Theory of the Individual in Social Relationship* (Cambridge: CUP, 1990).

Moltmann, Jürgen, *Man: Christian Anthropology in the Conflicts of the Present* (trans. John Sturdy, London: SPCK, 1974).

Nellas, Panayiotis, *Deification in Christ: The Nature of the Human Person* (Crestwood, NY: St. Vladimir's Seminary Press, 1987).

Niebuhr, Reinhold, *The Nature and Destiny of Man* (vol. 1, New York: Scribner's, 1964).

Pannenberg, Wolfhart, *Anthropology in Theological Perspective* (trans. Matthew J. O'Connell, Edinburgh: T&T Clark, 1985).

Sherlock, Charles, *The Doctrine of Humanity* (Contours of Christian Theology, Gerald Bray, ed., Downers Grove, IL: InterVarsity Press, 1996).

Shults, F. LeRon, *Reforming Theological Anthropology: After the Philosophical Turn to Relationality* (vol. xiv, Grand Rapids, MI: Eerdmans, 2003).

Soulen, R. Kendall, and Linda Woodhead (eds), *God and Human Dignity* (Grand Rapids, MI: Eerdmans, 2006).

Stevenson, Leslie, and David L. Haberman, *Ten Theories of Human Nature. Seven Theories of Human Nature* (New York/ Oxford: OUP, 1998).

Van Huyssteen, Wentzel, *Alone in the World: Human Uniqueness in Science and Theology* (The Gifford Lectures, Grand Rapids, MI: Eerdmans, 2006).

Zizioulas, John D., *Being as Communion: Studies in Personhood and the Church* (Crestwood, NY: St. Vladimir's Seminary Press, 1985).

Resources for learning about the image of God

Cairns, David, *The Image of God in Man* (London: SCM, 1953).

Gonzalez, Michelle A., *Created in God's Image: An Introduction to Feminist Theological Anthropology* (Maryknoll, NY: Orbis, 2007).

Grenz, Stanley J., *The Social God and the Relational Self: A Trinitarian Theology of the Imago Dei* (Philadelphia: Westminster, 2001).

Hoekema, Anthony, *Created in God's Image* (Grand Rapids, MI: Eerdmans, 1986).

Hughes, Philip Edgcumbe, *The True Image: The Origin and Destiny of Man in Christ* (Eugene, OR: Wipf and Stock, 2001).

McFarland, Ian A., *The Divine Image: Envisioning the Invisible God* (Minneapolis, MN: Fortress, 2005).

Middleton, J. Richard, *The Liberating Image: The Imago Dei in Genesis 1* (Grand Rapids, MI: Brazos, 2005).

Smail, Thomas Allan, *Like Father, Like Son: The Trinity Imaged in Our Humanity* (Grand Rapids, MI: Eerdmans, 2006).

Resources for learning about human sexuality

Balswick, Judith K., and Jack O. Balswick, *Authentic Human Sexuality: An Integrated Christian Approach* (2nd ed., Downers Grove, IL: IVP Academic, 2008).

Campbell, Douglas Atchison, and Alan J. Torrance, *Gospel and Gender: A Trinitarian Engagement with Being Male and Female in Christ* (Studies in Theology and Sexuality, London: T&T Clark, 2003).

Carr, Anne, and Elisabeth Schüssler Fiorenza (eds), *The Special Nature of Women?* (London: SCM, 1991).

Eagly, Alice H., Anne E. Beall, and Robert J. Sternberg (eds), *The Psychology of Gender* (2nd ed., New York: Guilford, 2004).

Graff, Ann Elizabeth O'Hara (ed.), *In the Embrace of God: Feminist Approaches to Theological Anthropology* (Maryknoll, NY: Orbis, 1995).

Graham, Elaine L., *Making the Difference: Gender, Personhood and Theology* (Minneapolis, MN: Fortress, 1996).

Jewett, Paul K., *Man as Male and Female: A Study in Sexual Relationships from a Theological Point of View* (Grand Rapids, MI: Eerdmans, 1975).

Lippa, Richard A., *Gender, Nature, and Nurture* (2nd ed., Mahwah, NJ: Lawrence Erlbaum Associates, 2005).

Nelson, James B., *Embodiment: An Approach to Sexuality and Christian Theology* (Minneapolis, MN: Augsburg, 1978).
Van Leeuwen, Mary Stewart, *My Brother's Keeper: What the Social Sciences Do (and Don't) Tell Us about Masculinity* (Downers Grove, IL: InterVarsity, 2002).

Resources for learning about the mind/body relationship

Brown, Warren S., Nancey C. Murphy, and H. Newton Malony (eds), *Whatever Happened to the Soul? Scientific and Theological Portraits of Human Nature* (Minneapolis, MN: Fortress, 1998).
Cooper, John W., *Body, Soul, and Life Everlasting* (Grand Rapids, MI: Eerdmans, 2000).
Corcoran, Kevin, *Rethinking Human Nature: A Christian Materialist Alternative to the Soul* (Grand Rapids, MI: Baker Academic, 2006).
Gazzaniga, Michael S., *Conversations in the Cognitive Neurosciences* (Cambridge, MA: MIT Press, 1997).
Gergersen, Niels Henrik, Willem B. Drees, and Ulf Gorman (eds), *Human Person in Science and Theology* (London: T&T Clark, 2000).
Green, Joel B., *What about the Soul? Neuroscience and Christian Anthropology* (Nashville: Abingdon, 2004).
Green, Joel B., Stuart L. Palmer, and Kevin Corcoran (eds), *In Search of the Soul: Four Views of the Mind–Body Problem* (Downers Grove, IL: InterVarsity, 2005).
Hasker, William, *The Emergent Self* (Ithaca, NY: Cornell University Press, 1999).
Jeeves, Malcolm, *From Cells to Souls—and Beyond: Changing Portraits of Human Nature* (Grand Rapids, MI: Eerdmans, 2004).
Moreland, J. P., and Scott B. Rae, *Body & Soul: Human Nature and the Crisis in Ethics* (Downers Grove, IL: InterVarstiy Press, 2000).
Murphy, Nancey, *Bodies and Souls, or Spirited Bodies: Human Nature at the Intersection* (David Ford Bryan Spinks Kathryn Tanner Iain Torrance and John Webster (eds), Cambridge: CUP, 2006).
Swinburne, Richard, *The Evolution of the Soul* (Oxford: Clarendon, 1986).
Taliaferro, Charles, *Consciousness and the Mind of God* (Cambridge: CUP, 1994).

Resources for learning about free will

Dennett, Daniel Clement, *Freedom Evolves* (New York: Viking, 2003).
Feinberg, John S., *No One Like Him: The Doctrine of God* (Wheaton, IL: Crossway, 2006).
Fischer, John Martin (ed.), *Four Views on Free Will* (Great Debates in Philosophy; Oxford: Blackwell, 2007).
Frame, John M., *The Doctrine of God* (A Theology of Lordship, Phillipsburg, NJ: P&R Pub., 2002).

Helm, Paul, *The Providence of God* (Contours of Christian Theology, Downers Grove, IL: InterVarsity Press, 1994).
Kane, Robert, *A Contemporary Introduction to Free Will* (Oxford: Oxford University Press, 2005).
Kane, Robert (ed.), *The Oxford Handbook of Free Will* (Oxford: Oxford University Press, 2001).
O'Connor, Timothy, *Persons and Causes: The Metaphysics of Free Will* (Oxford: Oxford University Press, 2000).
Tiessen, Terrance L., *Providence & Prayer: How Does God Work in the World?* (Downers Grove, IL: InterVarsity Press, 2000).
Ware, Bruce A., *God's Greater Glory: The Exalted God of Scripture and the Christian Faith* (Wheaton, IL: Crossway, 2004).

NOTES

1. INTRODUCTION

[1] Jürgen Moltmann, *Man: Christian Anthropology in the Conflicts of the Present*, trans. John Sturdy (London: SPCK, 1974), p. 1.

[2] G. C. Berkouwer, *Man: The Image of God* (Grand Rapids, MI: Eerdmans, 1962), p. 9.

[3] The contemporary struggle to answer the "Who am I?" question is born out in a number of recent movies that all deal with the loss and attempted recovery of one's personal identity (e.g., *Memento*, *The Bourne Identity*, *Eternal Sunshine of the Spotless Mind*, *Hancock*).

[4] Moltmann, *Man*, pp. 1–2.

[5] It might be tempting to think that these questions can be addressed sequentially—moving from ontology, to ethics, and finally to personal identity. On the contrary, the answer to each influences our understanding of the other, and we most commonly address the questions in precisely the opposite direction—moving from my understanding of my own identity in the world to a perspective on how humans ought to be in the world and finally to a view on what it fundamentally means to be human. Consequently, an adequate understanding of the human person should offer a satisfying way of engaging and understanding the human in response to all three of these questions.

[6] Christoph Schwöbel, "Recovering Human Dignity," in R. Kendall Soulen and Linda Woodhead (eds.), *God and Human Dignity* (Grand Rapids, MI: Eerdmans, 2006), pp. 44–59 (45). Indeed, Schwöbel goes further and argues that because different understandings of human ontology are ultimately based on theological considerations, "The debate between different anthropologies is therefore a debate of different (mostly implicit) theologies. One could almost claim that one needs to turn Feuerbach's projectionism from its head onto its feet" (Schwöbel, "Recovering Human Dignity," p. 46).

[7] Wolfhart Pannenberg, *Anthropology in Theological Perspective* (London: T&T Clark, 1985), p. 12.

[8] Pannenberg thus warns against an "anthropological bracketing of theology," even as he argues for the importance of theological anthropology (Pannenberg, *Anthropology in Theological Perspective*, p. 15).

[9] Berkouwer, *Man: The Image of God*, p. 23.

[10] Karl Barth, *Church Dogmatics* (London: T&T Clark 2004), III/2 136. Indeed, the WCC indicates this as an area of broad consensus among Christian theologians (*Christian Perspectives on Theological Anthropology: A Faith and Order Study Document* (Geneva: World Council of Churches, 2005), p. 48.

[11] Pannenberg, *Anthropology in Theological Perspective*, p. 18.

[12] Kathryn Tanner, "The Difference Theological Anthropology Makes," *Theology Today* 50 (1994), p. 567 (568).

[13] Berkouwer, *Man: The Image of God*, p. 18.

[14] Berkouwer, *Man: The Image of God*, p. 13.

2. IMAGO DEI

[1] Terms such as "person," "personhood," and "personal" as well as related terms such as "self" and "selfhood" are notoriously difficult to define and subject to strong cultural influences (see Charles Taylor, *Sources of the Self* (Cambridge: CUP, 1989); Stanley J. Grenz, *The Social God and the Relational Self: A Trinitarian Theology of the Imago Dei* (Philadelphia: Westminster, 2001); Philip A. Rolnick, *Person, Grace, and God* (Grand Rapids, MI: Eerdmans, 2007). Throughout this chapter, I will be using such terms in a rather loose manner to refer to the attributes that we associate with being able to engage in "meaningful" relationships and the beings that we associate with those attributes.

[2] Anthony Hoekema, *Created in God's Image* (Grand Rapids, MI: Eerdmans, 1986), p. 11.

[3] C. Clifton Black, "God's Promise for Humanity in the New Testament," in R. Kendall Soulen and Linda Woodhead (eds), *God and Human Dignity* (Grand Rapids, MI: Eerdmans, 2006), pp. 179–95 (180).

[4] For example, Irenaeus viewed the "image" as the capacity for rationality that distinguishes humans from other animals and continues to be exercised by humans after the fall; "likeness," on the other hand, is the "spirit" created in the human person by the Holy Spirit that places a "robe of sanctity" on the person and allows the human person to have fellowship with God (cf. *Against Heresies* 2.33.5; 3.23.5; 4.4.3; see also Aquinas *Summa Theologica* Iq93a9).

[5] Stanley J. Grenz, *The Social God and the Relational Self: A Trinitarian Theology of the Imago Dei* (Philadelphia: Westminster, 2001), pp. 186–89.

[6] Thus, according to Irenaeus, the human person is a being "endowed with reason, and in this respect like to God" (*Against Heresies* 5.6.1). Similarly, Gregory of Nyssa defined the human person as a "rational animal" and, thus, identified reason as the essence of the *imago* (*Of the Making of Man* 8.8).

[7] For example, Aquinas *Summa Theologica* Iq93a2.

[8] See, for example, Christopher L. Fisher, "Animals, Humans and X-Men: Human Uniqueness and the Meaning of Personhood," *Theology & Science* 3.3 (2005), pp. 291–314.

[9] Karl Barth, *Church Dogmatics* (London: T&T Clark, 2004), pp. III/1, 193.

[10] Thus, many recent studies demonstrate that we should understand our differences from other animals as being differences of degree (e.g., Anna Case-Winters, "Rethinking the Image of God," *Zygon* 39.4 (2004), pp. 813–26; Wentzel Van Huyssteen, *Alone in the World: Human Uniqueness in Science and Theology*, The Gifford Lectures (Grand Rapids, MI: Eerdmans, 2006). This does not mean, however, that we need to downplay the differences. Indeed, some have argued that even though humans share their capacities with the other animals, the differences in how those capacities are developed and expressed in human persons are significant enough to be viewed as differences in kind (e.g., Fisher, "Animals, Humans and X-Men"; Francisco J. Ayala, "Human Nature: One Evolutionist's View," in Warren S. Brown, Nancey Murphy, and H. Newton Maloney (eds), *Whatever Happened to the Soul? Scientific and Theological Portraits of Human Nature* (Minneapolis, MN: Fortress, 1998), pp. 31–48). The safest conclusion at this point is to emphasize humanity's commonality with and uniqueness within creation.

[11] Although it might be possible to define terms such as "self-transcendence" and "spirituality" in ways that would preclude any commonality with other animals, I would argue that this can only be done by subtly shifting the discussion from the "capacities" possessed by the human person to some "activity" engaged in by the person based on those capacities. That is, something like "spirituality" is distinct to the human person not because the human person has a set of spiritual capacities (what would those be anyway?) but because the human utilizes normal creaturely capacities while participating in spiritual activities (e.g., worship, prayer, ecclesial communion) (cf. Warren S. Brown, "Neurobiological Embodiment of Spirituality and Soul," in Malcolm Jeeves (ed.), *From Cells to Souls—and Beyond: Changing Portraits of Human Nature* (Grand Rapids, MI: Eerdmans, 2004), pp. 58–76.

[12] World Council of Churches, *Christian Perspectives on Theological Anthropology* (Geneva: World Council of Churches, 2005), p. 23.

[13] This is evident in the NT as well with its emphasis on the corporate body of the church being brought into unity and conformity with the person of Christ (see Grenz, *The Social God*, p. 201).

[14] See esp. Michael S. Gazzaniga, *Nature's Mind: The Biological Roots of Thinking, Sexuality, Language and Intelligence* (New York: Basic, 1992) and Joseph E. LeDoux, *The Emotional Brain: The Mysterious Underpinnings of Emotional Life* (New York: Simon & Schuster, 1996).

[15] This approach can be seen as far back as Aquinas, who made a distinction between the *imago* as an intellectual capacity and the *imago* as intellectual activity (i.e., knowing God) (*Summa Theologica* Iq93). Nonetheless, this approach did not become prominent until the modern era.

[16] Thus VanHuysteen argues, "In view of the extrabiblical evidence, the theme of the human domination of creation in Genesis 1:26, 28 and the wider context of Psalm 8:5, 6 . . . it is most natural to accept the idea of ruling or dominion as an important aspect of image and likeness, and not as something incidental" (*Alone in the World*, p. 102).

[17] Although theologians like Calvin and Luther set the stage for a relational understanding of the imago, Luther's emphasis on original righteousness and Calvin's continued use of more structural language somewhat obscures the fundamentally relational nature of their anthropologies. Consequently, it remained for later theologians to develop this approach more clearly.

[18] For example, Grenz, *The Social God*; Kathryn Tanner, "The Difference Theological Anthropology Makes," *Theology Today* 50.4 (1994), pp. 567–80; Paul K. Jewett and Marguerite Shuster, *Who We Are: Our Dignity as Human* (Grand Rapids, MI: Eerdmans, 1996); Ray S. Anderson, "On Being Human: The Spiritual Saga of a Creaturely Soul," in Warren S. Brown, Nancey Murphy, and H. Newton Malony (eds), *Whatever Happened to the Soul? Scientific and Theological Portraits of Human Nature* (Minneapolis, MN: Fortress, 1998), pp. 175–94.

[19] Barth, *Church Dogmatics*, III/1, 198.

[20] See, for example, Paul K. Jewett, *Man as Male and Female: A Study in Sexual Relationships from a Theological Point of View* (Grand Rapids, MI: Eerdmans, 1975); Alistair McFadyen, *The Call to Personhood: A Christian Theory of the Individual in Social Relationship* (Cambridge: CUP, 1990).

[21] Barth, *Church Dogmatics*, pp. III/1, 195.

[22] Barth, *Church Dogmatics*, pp. III/1, 196.

[23] James Barr, *Biblical Faith and Natural Theology: The Gifford Lectures for 1991* (Oxford: Clarendon, 1994), p. 160.

[24] See Nathan MacDonald, "*The Imago Dei* and Election: Reading Genesis 1:26–28 and Old Testament Scholarship with Karl Barth," *International Journal of Systematic Theology* 10.3 (2008), pp. 303–27.

[25] Bird, Phyllis, "Male and Female He Created Them": Gen 1.27b in the Context of the Priestly Account of Creation," *Harvard Theological Review* 74 (1981), p. 132.

[26] Grenz, *The Social God*, p. 200.

[27] MacDonald, "The *Imago Dei* and Election," p. 305.

[28] Grenz, *The Social God*, p. 198.

[29] It is important that we realize that human persons are constituted first by their relationship with God and only subsequently by their relationship with other human persons. As Christoph Schwöbel argues, "Human dignity is threatened where it is not understood as a dignity conferred upon humans by God in a creative divine act. . . . Human dignity becomes a social construct that is constituted in interpersonal relationships. . . . If it is constituted in this way, however, it can also be denied and destroyed in this way" (Christoph Schwöbel, "Recovering Human Dignity," in R. Kendall Soulen and Linda Woodhead (eds), *God and Human Dignity* (Grand Rapids, MI: Eerdmans, 2006), pp. 44–59 (53)).

[30] McFadyen, *The Call to Personhood*, p. 18. Thus, Michael Horton points out that throughout he biblical narratives there is a pattern of divine summons and human response that constitutes the self as "a situated, narrated subject" (Michael S. Horton, "Post-Reformation Reformed Anthropology," in Richard Lints, Michael S. Horton, and Mark R. Talbot

(eds), *Personal Identity in Theological Perspective* (Grand Rapids, MI: Eerdmans, 2006), pp. 45–69 (202).

[31] Allan M. Harman, *"Ezer,"* in William A. VanGemeren (ed.), *New International Dictionary of New Testament Theology & Exegesis* (Grand Rapids, MI: Zondervan, 1997), pp. 378–79.

[32] McFadyen, *The Call to Personhood*, p. 19.

[33] The question of how sexual differentiation relates to the manifestation of personal presence will have to wait until the next chapter.

[34] Barth, *Church Dogmatics*, pp. III/1, 181–82.

[35] Nathan MacDonald thus rightly points out that discussions of the *imago Dei* have unfortunately neglected the narratival unfolding of the *imago* in the history of God's dealings with Israel (MacDonald, "The *Imago Dei* and Election").

[36] Michael S. Horton, "Image and Office: Human Personhood and the Covenant," in Richard Lints, Michael S. Horton, and Mark R. Talbot (eds), *Personal Identity in Theological Perspective* (Grand Rapids, MI: Eerdmans, 2006), pp. 178–203 (181).

[37] Grenz, *The Social God*, p. 279.

[38] Robert W. Jenson, *"Anima Ecclesiastica,"* in R. Kendall Soulen and Linda Woodhead (eds), *God and Human Dignity* (Grand Rapids, MI: Eerdmans, 2006), pp. 59–71 (67).

[39] Cf. Marc Cortez, *Embodied Souls, Besouled Bodies: An Exercise in Christological Anthropology and Its Significance for the Mind/Body Debate*, John Webster, Ian McFarland, and Ivor Davidson (eds), T&T Clark Studies in Systematic Theology (London: T&T Clark, 2008).

[40] John Macquarrie, *In Search of Humanity: A Theological and Philosophical Approach* (New York: Crossroad, 1983), p. 6.

[41] See Christoph Schwöbel, "Human Being as Relational Being: Twelve Theses for a Christian Anthropology," in Christoph Schwöbel and Colin E. Gunton (eds), *Persons, Divine, and Human* (London: T&T Clark, 1991), pp. 141–65.

[42] Thus, the functional/relational approach does not completely reject the insights of the structural approach, but it does serve to place structural considerations within a broader framework. Structural capacities do not *define* the image, but they are certainly involved in how we *express* the image.

3. SEXUALITY

[1] Derrick Sherwin Bailey, *Sexual Relation in Christian Thought* (New York: Harper, 1959), pp. 280–81.

[2] Jewett, Paul K. and Marguerite Shuster, *Man as Male and Female: A Study in Sexual Relationships from a Theological Point of View* (Grand Rapids, MI: Eerdmans, 1975), p. 172

[3] Judith K. Balswick and Jack O. Balswick, *Authentic Human Sexuality: An Integrated Christian Approach*, 2nd ed. (Downers Grove, IL: IVP Academic, 2008), p. 13.

⁴ Because this chapter will focus primarily on understanding the nature of human sexuality, the limitations of space will prevent us from also exploring the pressing practical questions that arise as we live our sexuality in the world. This is unfortunate if it causes us to think that we can understand sexuality in abstraction from these daily realities. What we have in this chapter is just the beginning of a discussion on human sexuality, the continuation of which would require a more direct engagement with these practical issues.

⁵ Although the text refers to "male and female" right away, this reference serves to declare that all human persons, who are now sexually differentiated, share in this common human essence that regardless of their sexuality.

⁶ Gregory of Nyssa, *On the Making of Man*, 16.

⁷ Nikolai Berdyaev, *The Destiny of Man*, trans. Natalie Duddington (Westport, CT: Hyperion, 1979), pp. 61–67.

⁸ Gregory of Nyssa, *On the Making of Man*, 17.2

⁹ Alice H. Eagly, Anne E. Beall, and Robert J. Sternberg, "Introduction," in Alice H. Eagly, Anne E. Beall, and Robert J. Sternberg (eds), *The Psychology of Gender* (New York: Guilford, 2004), pp. 1–8 (1).

¹⁰ World Council of Churches, *Christian Perspectives on Theological Anthropology: A Faith and Order Study Document* (Geneva: World Council of Churches, 2005), p. 37.

¹¹ Simone de Beauvoir, *The Second Sex*, trans. H. M. Parshley (Franklin Center, PA: Franklin Library, 1953), p. 83.

¹² Aristotle, *On the Generation of Animals*, 2.3; cf. also Aquinas, *Summa Theologica* I.q92.a1.

¹³ Emil Brunner, *Man in Revolt, a Christian Anthropology* (Philadelphia: Westminster, 1947), p. 345.

¹⁴ Grenz, Stanley J., *The Social God and the Relational Self: A Trinitarian Theology of the* Imago Dei (Philadelphia: Westminster, 2001), p. 277.

¹⁵ Mary Stewart Van Leeuwen, *My Brother's Keeper: What the Social Sciences Do (and Don't) Tell Us about Masculinity* (Downers Grove, IL: InterVarsity Press, 2002), pp. 73–76.

¹⁶ For example, Elizabeth Hampson and Scott D. Moffat, "The Psychobiology of Gender: Cognitive Effects of Reproductive Hormones in the Adult Nervous System," in Alice H. Eagly, Anne E. Beall, and Robert J. Sternberg (eds), *The Psychology of Gender* (New York: Guilford, 2004), pp. 38–64; Melissa Hines, "Androgen, Estrogen, and Gender: Contributions of the Early Hormone Environment to Gender-Related Behavior," in Alice H. Eagly, Anne E. Beall, and Robert J. Sternberg (eds), *The Psychology of Gender* (New York: Guilford, 2004), pp. 9–37.

¹⁷ Hines, "Androgen, Estrogen, and Gender," p. 10.

¹⁸ For example, Anne Moir and David Jessel, *Brain Sex: The Real Difference between Men and Women* (New York: Carol, 1991); David P. Barash, Judith Eve Lipton, and David P. Barash, *Gender Gap: The Biology of Male–Female Differences* (New Brunswick, NJ: Transaction, 2002). Another key line of argument not typically cited by theologically inclined essentialists is that of evolutionary psychology, which contends that

gender differences are rooted in evolutionary adaptations that have accrued over the millennia. The argument that evolutionary psychology can account for specific differences, however, is highly debated and, since it does not factor prominently into the debate in theological circles, we will not address its arguments in this chapter.

[19] See especially the studies in Richard A. Lippa, *Gender, Nature, and Nurture*, 2nd ed. (Mahwah, NJ: Lawrence Erlbaum Associates, 2005).

[20] For example, Wayne A. Grudem, *Systematic Theology: An Introduction to Biblical Doctrine* (Grand Rapids, MI: Zondervan, 1994), p. 459ff.

[21] Lippa, *Gender, Nature, and Nurture*, p. 68.

[22] Beauvoir, *The Second Sex*, p. 18.

[23] The term "gender" was originally used to refer solely to masculine and feminine words. It was only in the 1960s that it was used in conjunction with "sex" as a way of distinguishing biological and cultural influences in human sexuality.

[24] L. Nicholson, "Interpreting Gender," *Signs* 20 (1994), pp. 79–105 (81).

[25] Mari Mikkola, "Feminist Perspectives on Sex and Gender," in Edward N. Zalta (ed.), *Stanford Encyclopedia of Philosophy* (accessed September 19, 2008; <http://plato.stanford.edu/archives/fall2008/entries/feminism-gender/>).

[26] Jeanne Marecek, Mary Crawford, and Danielle Popp, "On the Construction of Gender, Sex, and Sexualities," in Alice H. Eagly, Anne E. Beall, and Robert J. Sternberg (eds), *The Psychology of Gender* (New York: Guilford, 2004), pp. 192–216 (201).

[27] See Christine Gorman and J. Madeleine Nash, "Sizing up the Sexes," *Time* 139.3 (1992), p. 42.

[28] See in particular Anne Fausto-Sterling, *Sexing the Body: Gender Politics and the Construction of Sexuality* (New York: Basic Books, 2000).

[29] Hampson and Moffat, "The Psychobiology of Gender," p. 59.

[30] Van Leeuwen, *My Brother's Keeper*, p. 79ff.

[31] This condition occurs in approximately 0.005% of the population, or nearly 340,000 people.

[32] See Lippa, *Gender, Nature, and Nurture*, pp. 122ff.

[33] Eagly, Beall, and Sternberg, "Introduction," p. 1.

[34] For example, the "Two-Spirit" people among some Native Americans, the Hijra in India and Pakistan, the Kathoey in Thailand, and the "transgendered" in modern western society.

[35] Heather Looy and Hessel III Bouma, "The Nature of Gender: Gender Identity in Persons Who Are Intersexed or Transgendered," *Journal of Psychology and Theology* 33.3 (2005), pp. 166–78 (166).

[36] Mikkola, "Feminist Perspectives on Sex and Gender."

[37] Van Leeuwen, *My Brother's Keeper*, p. 25.

[38] Judith Butler, *Gender Trouble: Feminism and the Subversion of Identity* (New York: Routledge, 1999).

[39] We could retain some of the language of thoroughgoing constructivism if we expanded our notion of "social" to include the society of relationship that exists between God and humans. Doing so, however, would superficially retain the language of constructivism while rejecting its basic framework.

[40] Eagly, Beall, and Sternberg, "Introduction," p. 4. The real argument is not in whether there are differences but understanding the source and nature of these differences.

[41] John Gray, *Men Are from Mars, Women Are from Venus: A Practical Guide for Improving Communication and Getting What You Want in Your Relationships* (New York: HarperCollins, 1992).

[42] Dorothy L. Sayers, "The Human-not-Quite-Human," *Are Women Human?* (Grand Rapids, MI: Eerdmans, 2005), pp. 51–69 (53).

[43] Van Leeuwen, *My Brother's Keeper*, p. 28.

[44] Eagly, Beall, and Sternberg, "Introduction," p. 4.

[45] See Lippa, *Gender, Nature, and Nurture*, esp. chapter 4.

[46] Van Leeuwen, *My Brother's Keeper*, p. 10.

[47] James B. Nelson, *Embodiment: An Approach to Sexuality and Christian Theology* (Minneapolis, MN: Augsburg, 1978), p. 102.

[48] Jewett, Paul K., and Shuster, M., *Who We Are: Our Dignity as Human: A Neo-Evangelical Theology* (Grand Rapids, MI: Eerdmans, 1996), p. 177.

[49] Michelle A. Gonzalez, *Created in God's Image: An Introduction to Feminist Theological Anthropology* (Maryknoll, NY: Orbis, 2007), p. 136.

[50] Heather Looy, and Hessel III Bouma, "The Nature of Gender: Gender Identity in Persons Who Are Intersexed or Transgendered," *Journal of Psychology and Theology* 33.3 (2005), pp. 166–78 (173).

[51] Lippa, *Gender, Nature, and Nurture*, p. 223.

[52] *On Marriage and Concupiscence*, 5.

[53] *On Marriage and Concupiscence*, 7.

[54] Catholic Church, *Catechism of the Catholic Church*, Rev. ed. (London: Geoffrey Chapman, 1999), par. 372. We will see shortly that many Catholic theologians actually have a broader understanding of the nature of sexuality than this might suggest. Nonetheless, procreation remains a prominent aspect of the typically Catholic view of sexuality.

[55] Grenz, *The Social God*, p. 273.

[56] Luce Irigaray, *An Ethics of Sexual Difference* (Ithaca, NY: Cornell University Press, 1993), p. 5.

[57] Jewett and Shuster, *Who We Are*, p. 131.

[58] Barth, *Church Dogmatics*, pp. III/1, 198.

[59] Barth, *Church Dogmatics*, pp. III/4, 166.

[60] Alistair Iain McFadyen, *The Call to Personhood: A Christian Theory of the Individual in Social Relationships* (Cambridge: Cambridge University Press, 1990), pp. 31–32.

[61] McFadyen, *The Call to Personhood*, p. 36.

[62] Grenz, *The Social God*, p. 276.

[63] Grenz, *The Social God*, p. 277.

[64] Grenz, *The Social God*, p. 274.

[65] Grenz, *The Social God*, p. 278.

[66] Grenz, *The Social God*, p. 279.

[67] Grenz, *The Social God*, p. 280.

[68] Grenz, *The Social God*, p. 279.

[69] Nelson, *Embodiment*, p. 18.

70 Grenz, *The Social God*, p. 281.
71 Thus, Gregory of Nyssa viewed sexual reproduction as the means established by God for the continuation of the human community despite the fall.

4. MIND AND BODY

1 For the purposes of this study, I will use the terms "mind" and "soul" interchangeably.
2 Graham McFarlane, "Review of Niels Henrik Gregersen, *The Human Person in Science and Theology* (London: T&T Clark, 2000), *Science and Christian Belief* 14 (2002), pp. 94–95.
3 Cf. Robert Jewett, *Paul's Anthropological Terms* (Leiden: Brill, 1971); Hans Walter Wolff, *Anthropology of the Old Testament* (London: SCM, 1974).
4 For example, Jaegwon Kim, *Supervenience and Mind: Selected Philosophical Essays* (Cambridge: CUP, 1993).
5 For example, Paul M. Churchland, "Eliminative Materialism and Propositional Attitudes," *Journal of Philosophy* 78 (1981), pp. 67–90.
6 For useful summaries of some of these developments see Malcolm Jeeves, "Mind Reading and Soul Searching in the Twenty-First Century: The Scientific Evidence," in Joel B. Green (ed.), *What about the Soul? Neuroscience and Christian Anthropology* (Nashville, TN: Abingdon, 2004), pp. 13–30.
7 For example, Moreland, J. P., and Scott B. Rae, *Body & Soul: Human Nature and the Crisis in Ethics* (Downers Grove, IL: InterVarsity, 2000)., p. 17.
8 We must emphasize, however, that dualism need only affirm the *conceivability* of such ontological separation and not necessarily its *actuality*.
9 John W. Cooper, *Body, Soul, and Life Everlasting* (Grand Rapids, MI: Eerdmans, 2000), p. 45.
10 For example, Karl Popper, *Knowledge and the Body–Mind Problem: In Defense of Interaction* (London: Routledge, 1994); William Hasker, *The Emergent Self* (Ithaca: Cornell University Press, 1999).
11 Hasker, *The Emergent Self*, p. 189.
12 Hasker, *The Emergent Self*, pp. 189–90.
13 For example, David Braine, *The Human Person: Animal and Spirit* (Notre Dame: University of Notre Dame Press, 1992); Eleanore Stump, "Non-Cartesian Substance Dualism and Materialism without Reductionism," *Faith and Philosophy* 12 (1995), pp. 505–31.
14 Eleanore Stump, "Non-Cartesian Substance Dualism and Materialism without Reductionism," *Faith and Philosophy* 12 (1995), pp. 505–31 (508); cf. Aquinas, *Summa Theologica* Ia.76.1.
15 Moreland and Rae, *Body & Soul*, p. 202.
16 Charles Taliaferro, *Consciousness and the Mind of God* (Cambridge: CUP, 1994), p. 568.

[17] Jaegwon Kim, "Lonely Souls: Causality and Substance Dualism," in Kevin Corcoran (ed.), *Soul, Body, and Survival: Essays on the Metaphysics of Human Persons* (Ithaca: Cornell University Press, 2001), pp. 30–43 (32).

[18] Cf. particularly John Foster, "Psychophysical Causal Relations," *American Philosophical Quarterly* 5.1 (1968), pp. 64–70.

[19] Joshua Hoffman and Gary S. Rosenkrantz, *Substance: Its Nature and Existence* (London New York: Routledge, 1997), p. 197.

[20] Jaegwon Kim, "Supervenience," in Hans Burkhardt and Barry Smith (eds), *Handbook of Metaphysics and Ontology* (Munich, Philadelphia: Philosophia Verlag, 1991), pp. 119–38 (250).

[21] Peter Atkins, "Purposeless People," in Arthur Peacocke and Grant Gillett (eds), *Persons and Personality: A Contemporary Inquiry* (Oxford: Basil Blackwell, 1987), pp. 12–32 (13).

[22] Apparently this objection was first formulated by Leibniz (Edward Averill and B. F. Keating, "Does Interactionism Violate a Law of Classical Physics?" *Mind* 90.357 (1981), pp. 102–07).

[23] Robert Larmer, "Mind–Body Interaction and the Conservation of Energy," *International Philosophical Quarterly* 26 (1986), pp. 277–85 (277).

[24] Karl R. Popper and John Carew Eccles, *The Self and Its Brain: An Argument for Interactionism* (New York: Springer International, 1977).

[25] For example, Averill and Keating, "Does Interactionism Violate a Law of Classical Physics?"

[26] Some have argued that quantum science provides support for the idea that physical systems are not "hermetically sealed off from 'outside' forces" (Taliaferro, *Consciousness and the Mind of God*, p. 221). Whether such appeals to quantum mechanics can provide the necessary support for dualist causation, though, would require a far more extensive understanding and analysis of quantum theory than is possible in this chapter and, indeed, than is normally offered by dualists appealing to it (though cf. Roger Penrose, *The Emperor's New Mind* (Oxford: OUP, 1989)).

[27] Although the Cartesian dualist could posit some nonspatial relation to individuate souls or some other metaphysically deep but epistemologically unavailable principle of individuation (e.g., haecceity), they have yet to provide a meaningful explanation of what such an account might be.

[28] Jaegwon Kim, "The Non-Reductivist's Troubles with Mental Causation," in John Heil and Alfred R. Mele (eds), *Mental Causation* (Oxford: Clarendon, 1993), pp. 189–210 (190).

[29] Jaegwon Kim, "The Mind–Body Problem after Fifty Years," *Royal Institute of Philosophy Supplement* 43 (1998), pp. 3–21 (7).

[30] Kim, "The Mind–Body Problem after Fifty Years," p. 10.

[31] For a good overview of emergence and its historical development see Ansgar Beckermann, H. Flohr, and Jaegwon Kim, *Emergence or Reduction? Prospects of Nonreductive Physicalism* (Berlin: Walter de Gruyter, 1992).

[32] These labels come from John R. Searle, *The Rediscovery of Mind* (Cambridge, Mass: MIT Press, 1992). Since many question whether

*emergent*₂ qualifies as a truly physicalist ontology, suspecting that it is actually a form of dualism in disguise, we will focus in this chapter on *emergent*₁.

[33] Lynne Rudder Baker, "Why Constitution Is not Identity," *Journal of Philosophy* 94.1 (1997), pp. 599–621.

[34] For example, Michael E. Levin, *Metaphysics and the Mind–Body Problem* (Oxford: Clarendon, 1979); There are some, however, who argue that physicalism is actually the more intuitive approach (e.g., Peter van Inwagen, "Dualism and Materialism: Athens and Jerusalem?" *Faith and Philosophy* 12.4 (1995), pp. 475–88). In some ways, then, we are dealing with a conflict of basic intuitions that makes negotiating the various arguments quite difficult.

[35] John R. Searle, "Consciousness" (accessed 8 October 2005) http://humanities.ucsc.edu/NEH/searle1.htm

[36] Joseph Levine, "Materialism and Qualia: The Explanatory Gap," *Pacific Philosophical Quarterly* 64 (1983), pp. 354–415.

[37] Some thinkers, then, have proposed that all physical entities have intrinsic phenomenal properties (panpsychism) or that that physical and mental properties are properties of some fundamental substance that is itself neither mental nor physical (neutral monism).

[38] For example, Daniel Stoljar, "Physicalism and Phenomenal Concepts," *Mind and Language* 20 (2005), pp. 469–94.

[39] This is a modified form of the argument presented in Taliaferro, *Consciousness and the Mind of God*, p. 175.

[40] Constitution theorists, however, would differ on this point and would respond differently to this argument. Nonetheless, most physicalists affirm some kind of identity relationship between mind and body.

[41] See William Hasker, "Swinburne's Modal Argument for Dualism: Epistemically Circular," *Faith and Philosophy* 15.3 (1998), pp. 366–70; Stewart Goetz, "Modal Dualism: A Critique," in Kevin Corcoran (ed.), *Soul, Body, and Survival: Essays on the Metaphysics of Human Persons* (Ithaca, NY: Cornell University Press, 2001), pp. 89–104.

[42] Carsten Martin Hansen, "Between a Rock and a Hard Place: Mental Causation and the Mind-Body Problem," *Inquiry* 43.4 (2000), pp. 451–92 (470).

[43] By rejecting the possibility that the body as a materially composite entity could be the ground of personal identity, these thinkers all reject the classic "reassembly" version of the resurrection.

[44] Peter van Inwagen, "Possibility of Resurrection," *International Journal for Philosophy of Religion* 9.2 (1978), pp. 114–21.

[45] Kevin Corcoran, "Physical Persons and Postmortem Survival," in Kevin Corcoran (ed.), *Soul, Body, and Survival: Essays on the Metaphysics of Human Persons* (Ithaca, NY: Cornell University Press, 2001), pp. 201–17. Corcoran responds to the objection that that God could create multiple biological organisms who are all biologically continuous with the same person by simply stating that God would not participate in such an action. Though this certainly seems reasonable, it requires that we see

strict identity relationships as dependent on extrinsic factors—something typically held to be incompatible with strict identity (cf. Saul A. Kripke, "Identity and Necessity," in John Heil (ed.), *Philosophy of Mind: A Guide and Anthology* (Oxford: OUP, 2004), pp. 128–33). Van Inwagen's solution, though problematic as well, at least avoids this problem.

46 Although the intermediate state often factors into the discussion at this point, Lynn Baker rightly argues that an intermediate state by itself does not raise any issues for physicalist ontologies that do not already arise with respect to resurrection in general (Lynne Rudder Baker, "Need a Christian Be a Mind/Body Dualist?" *Faith and Philosophy* 12.4 (1995), pp. 489–504).

47 Cf. Trenton Merricks, "Endurance, Psychological Continuity, and the Importance of Personal Identity," *Philosophy and Phenomenological Research* 59 (1999), pp. 983–97.

48 For example, Trenton Merricks "There Are no Criteria of Identity over Time," *Nous* 32 (1998), pp. 106–24; Nancey Murphy, "The Resurrection Body and Personal Identity: Possibilities and Limits of Eschatological Knowledge," in Ted Peters, Robert J. Russell, and Michael Welker (eds), *Resurrection: Theological and Scientific Assessments* (Grand Rapids, MI: Eerdmans, 2002), pp. 202–18.

49 Daniel Dennett, *Brainstorms: Philosophical Essays on Mind and Psychology* (Montgomery, VT: Bradford, 1978).

50 Steven P. R. Rose, "Introduction: The New Brain Sciences," in David A. Rees and Steven P. R. Rose (eds), *The New Brain Sciences: Perils and Prospects* (New York: CUP, 2004), pp. 3–14 (5).

51 Kevin Corcoran, "Introduction," in Kevin Corcoran (ed.), *Soul, Body, and Survival: Essays on the Metaphysics of Human Persons* (Ithaca, NY: Cornell University Press, 2001), pp. 1–11 (11).

52 Among the classic older studies are Walther Eichrodt, *Man in the Old Testament*, trans. R. Gregor Smith (London: SCM, 1951); Werner Georg Kümmel, *Man in the New Testament*, trans. John J. Vincent (London: Epworth 1963); Jewett, *Paul's Anthropological Terms.*; Hans Walter Wolff, *Anthropology of the Old Testament*, trans. Margaret Kohl (London: SCM, 1974); and Robert H. Gundry, *Soma in Biblical Theology, with Emphasis on Pauline Anthropology* (Cambridge: CUP, 1976).

53 In a number of recent articles, Joel Green convincingly demonstrates and exemplifies the predominantly physicalist orientation of most contemporary biblical scholars (e.g., Joel B. Green, "Eschatology and the Nature of Humans: A Reconsideration of Pertinent Biblical Evidence," *Science & Christian Belief* 14.1 (2002), p. 33; a point that is not disputed by dualist biblical scholars.

54 Among the more recent relevant studies are Joseph Osei-Bonsu, "Anthropological Dualism in the New Testament," *Scottish Journal of Theology* 40.4 (1987), pp. 571–90; John W. Cooper, *Body, Soul, and Life Everlasting* (Grand Rapids, MI: Eerdmans, 2000); and N. T. Wright, *The Resurrection of the Son of God* (London: SPCK, 2003).

55 For example, Popper and Eccles, *The Self and Its Brain.*; Richard Swinburne, *The Evolution of the Soul* (Oxford: Clarendon, 1986); Taliaferro,

Consciousness and the Mind of God; Hasker, *The Emergent Self*; though cf. Moreland and Rae, *Body & Soul*; Goetz, "Substance Dualism."

56 Stephen T. Davis, "The Resurrection of the Dead," in Stephen T. Davis (ed.), *Death and Afterlife* (Basingstoke: Macmillan, 1989), pp. 119–44 (121).

57 One promising possibility here would be to appeal to the possibility that God could miraculously sustain some level of functionality for the mind during the intermediate state (cf. Hasker, *The Emergent Self*). Thus, the person continues to exist independently of the body, not because the mind is basically immortal and capable of functioning in a disembodied state, but because God chooses to mercifully sustain its existence until its eventual re-embodiment.

5. FREE WILL

1 Nikolai Berdyaev, *"Personality," Slavery and Freedom* (New York: Charles Scribner's Sons, 1944), pp. 20–59 (36).

2 This is true even for those theologians who affirm some form of theological determinism. Neither foreknowledge nor an eternal divine decree necessarily denies the significance of human action. Indeed, some of the theologians most associated with a strong view of God's sovereign plan (e.g., Augustine, Calvin) have also presented the human free will as tremendously vital and significant.

3 We will see however that one of the key difficulties of a theistic compatibilism is to explain how it avoids these concerns about manipulation and coercion given its construal of divine sovereignty and causality.

4 See Timothy O'Connor, "Free Will," in Edward N. Zalta (ed.), *The Stanford Encyclopedia of Philosophy* (Fall 2008 Edition) (accessed December 12, 2008; http://plato.stanford.edu/archives/fall2008/entries/freewill/).

5 Robert Kane, *A Contemporary Introduction to Free Will* (Oxford: OUP, 2005), p. 6. Thus, determinism is not significantly impacted by whether one views the determining conditions as fully natural (e.g., environmental, behavior, or biological determinism) or supernatural (i.e., theistic determinism). In either case, the system is determinative in that there is some condition that obtains prior (either temporally or logically) to the event and that makes it the case that the event will in fact occur.

6 Not all compatibilists affirm that determinism is in fact true; they simply maintain that determinism (if true) is fully compatible with free will.

7 Paul Helm, *The Providence of God*, Contours of Christian Theology (Downers Grove, IL: InterVarsity, 1994), p. 22.

8 Jonathan Edwards, *Freedom of the Will* (accessed March 6, 2009; http://www.ccel.org/ccel/edwards/will.html)

9 John M. Frame, *The Doctrine of God: A Theology of Lordship* (Phillipsburg, NJ: P&R, 2002), p. 62.

10 Frame, *The Doctrine of God*, p. 63. Of course, one does not have to view God as producing these desires directly. It is conceivable that God knows precisely how we would respond given different sets of influences; he could thus control our desires and character indirectly through his control

of our circumstances (cf. Bruce A. Ware, *God's Greater Glory: The Exalted God of Scripture and the Christian Faith* (Wheaton: Crossway, 2004)).

11 Daniel Dennett, *Elbow Room: The Varieties of Free Will Worth Wanting* (Cambridge, MA: MIT Press, 1984), p. 133.

12 For this summary, see Michael McKenna, "Compatibilism," in Edward N. Zalta (ed.), *The Stanford Encyclopedia of Philosophy* (Summer 2004 Edition*)* (accessed May 31, 2007; http://plato.stanford.edu/archives/fall2008/entries/compatibilism/).

13 Peter van Inwagen, *An Essay on Free Will* (New York: Clarendon, 1983).

14 O'Connor, "Free Will," in Edward N. Zalta (ed.), *The Stanford Encyclopedia of Philosophy* (Fall 2008 Edition) (accessed December 12, 2008; http://plato.stanford.edu/archives/fall2008/entries/freewill/).

15 Cf. Lynne Rudder Baker, "Moral Responsibility without Libertarianism," *Nous* 40 (2006), pp. 307–30.

16 For example, Ware, *God's Greater Glory*, p. 122.

17 John S. Feinberg, *No One Like Him: The Doctrine of God* (Wheaton: Crossway, 2006), p. 655.

18 Jonathan Edwards, *A Dissertation Concerning the End for Which God Made the World* (accessed January 4, 2009; http://www.ccel.org/ccel/edwards/works1.iv.html>

19 Cf. Helm, *The Providence of God*, p. 176.

20 Kane, *A Contemporary Introduction*, pp. 32–33.

21 Michael Polanyi, *Personal Knowledge: Towards a Post-Critical Philosophy* (Chicago,: University of Chicago Press, 1958), p. 309.

22 For example, Hugh McCann, *The Works of Agency: On Human Action, Will, and Freedom* (Ithaca, NY: Cornell University Press, 1998); Carl Ginet, "Reasons Explanations of Action: Causalist versus Noncausalist Accounts," in Robert Kane (ed.), *The Oxford Handbook of Free Will* (New York: Clarendon, 2002), pp. 386–405.

23 Kane, *A Contemporary Introduction*, p. 121.

24 Kane, *A Contemporary Introduction*, pp. 32–33.

25 Kane, *A Contemporary Introduction*, p. 46.

26 It is a matter of debate whether quantum physics entails that the universe is actually indeterminate or only that it appears so given the limitations of our current understanding.

27 Ware, *God's Greater Glory*, p. 25.

28 Alfred R. Mele and David Robb, "Rescuing Frankfurt-Style Cases," *Philosophical Review* 107 (1998), pp. 97–112.

29 Timothy O'Connor, *Persons and Causes: The Metaphysics of Free Will* (Oxford: Oxford University Press, 2000), p. 85.

30 O'Connor, *Persons and Causes*, p. 95.

31 O'Connor, *Persons and Causes*, p. 88.

32 Whether human persons can act in ways that are entirely irrational (i.e., completely disconnected from underlying reasons) is another question.

33 Baker, "Moral Responsibility," p. 313.

[34] Cf. Richard Swinburne, *The Christian God* (Oxford: Oxford University Press, 1994).

[35] Cf. William Hasker, *God, Time, and Knowledge* (Ithaca: Cornell University Press, 1989).

[36] Daniel C. Dennett, "Natural Freedom," *Metaphilosophy* 36.4 (2005), pp. 449–59 (455).

[37] Ted A. Warfield, "Causal Determinism and Human Freedom Are Incompatible: A New Argument for Incompatibilism," *Philosophical Perspectives* 14 (2000), pp. 167–80 (177).

[38] Feinberg, *No One Like Him*, p. 679.

[39] Jonathan Schaffer, "The Metaphysics of Causation," in Edward N. Zalta (ed.), *The Stanford Encyclopedia of Philosophy* (Fall 2008 edition) (accessed March 24, 2009; http://plato.stanford.edu/archives/fall2008/entries/causation-metaphysics/).

[40] David M. Ciocchi, "Suspending the Debate about Divine Sovereignty and Human Freedom," *Journal of the Evangelical Theological Society* 51.3 (2008), pp. 573–90.

6. CONCLUSION

[1] Charles Dickens, *A Tale of Two Cities* (New York: Penguin, 2000), p. 12.

BIBLIOGRAPHY

Anderson, Ray S., "On Being Human: The Spiritual Saga of a Creaturely Soul," in Warren S. Brown, Nancey Murphy and H. Newton Malony (eds), *Whatever Happened to the Soul? Scientific and Theological Portraits of Human Nature* (Augsburg Fortress, 1998), pp. 175–94.

Atkins, Peter, "Purposeless People," in Arthur Peacocke and Grant Gillett (eds), *Persons and Personality: A Contemporary Inquiry* (Oxford: Blackwell, 1987), pp. 12–32.

Averill, Edward, and B. F. Keating, "Does Interactionism Violate a Law of Classical Physics?" *Mind* 90.357 (1981), pp. 102–07.

Ayala, Francisco J., "Human Nature: One Evolutionist's View," in Warren S. Brown, Nancey Murphy and H. Newton Maloney (eds), *Whatever Happened to the Soul? Scientific and Theological Portraits of Human Nature* (Augsburg: Fortress, 1998), pp. 31–48.

Bailey, Derrick Sherwin, *Sexual Relation in Christian Thought* (New York: Harper, 1959).

Baker, Lynne Rudder, "Need a Christian Be a Mind/Body Dualist?" *Faith and Philosophy* 12.4 (1995), pp. 489–504.

—, "Why Constitution is not Identity," *Journal of Philosophy* 94.1 (1997), pp. 599–621.

Balswick, Judith K., and Jack O. Balswick, *Authentic Human Sexuality: An Integrated Christian Approach* (2nd ed., Downers Grove, IL: IVP Academic, 2008).

Barash, David P., Judith Eve Lipton, and David P. Barash, *Gender Gap: The Biology of Male–Female Differences* (New Brunswick, NJ: Transaction, 2002).

Barr, James, *Biblical Faith and Natural Theology: The Gifford Lectures for 1991* (Oxford: Clarendon, 1994).

Barth, Karl, *Church Dogmatics* (London: T&T Clark, 2004).

Beauvoir, Simone de, *The Second Sex* (trans. H. M. Parshley, Franklin Center, PA: Franklin Library, 1953).

Beckermann, Ansgar, H. Flohr, and Jaegwon Kim (eds), *Emergence or Reduction? Prospects of Nonreductive Physicalism* (Berlin: Walter de Gruyter, 1992).

Berdyaev, Nikolai, *The Destiny of Man* (trans. Natalie Duddington, Westport, CT.: Hyperion Press, 1979).

—, "Personality," in *Slavery and Freedom* (New York: Charles Scribner's Sons, 2001), pp. 20–59.

BIBLIOGRAPHY

Berkouwer, G. C., *Man: The Image of God* (Grand Rapids, MI: Eerdmans, 1962).

Bird, Phyllis, "'Male and Female He Created Them': Gen 1:27b in the Context of the Priestly Account of Creation," *Harvard Theological Review* 74 (1981), pp. 129–59.

Black, C. Clifton, "God's Promise for Humanity in the New Testament," in R. Kendall Soulen and Linda Woodhead (eds), *God and Human Dignity* (Grand Rapids, MI: Eerdmans, 2006), pp. 179–95.

Braine, David, *The Human Person: Animal and Spirit* (Notre Dame: University of Notre Dame Press, 1992).

Brown, Warren S., "Neurobiological Embodiment of Spirituality and Soul," in Malcolm Jeeves (ed.), *From Cells to Souls—and Beyond: Changing Portraits of Human Nature* (Grand Rapids, MI: Eerdmans, 2004), pp. 58–76.

Brown, Warren S., Nancey C. Murphy, and H. Newton Malony (eds), *Whatever Happened to the Soul?: Scientific and Theological Portraits of Human Nature* (Minneapolis, MN: Fortress, 1998).

Brunner, Emil, and Olive Wyon, *Man in Revolt, a Christian Anthropology* (Philadelphia: Westminster Press, 1947).

Butler, Judith, *Gender Trouble: Feminism and the Subversion of Identity* (New York: Routledge, 1999).

Churchland, Paul M., "Eliminative Materialism and Propositional Attitudes," *Journal of Philosophy* 78 (1981), pp. 67–90.

Ciocchi, David M., "Suspending the Debate About Divine Sovereignty and Human Freedom," *Journal of the Evangelical Theological Society* 51.3 (2008), pp. 573–90.

Cooper, John W., *Body, Soul, and Life Everlasting* (Grand Rapids, MI: Eerdmans, 2000).

Corcoran, Kevin, "Introduction," in Kevin Corcoran (ed.), *Soul, Body, and Survival: Essays on the Metaphysics of Human Persons* (Ithaca, NY: Cornell University Press, 2001), pp. 1–11.

—, "Physical Persons and Postmortem Survival," in Kevin Corcoran (ed.), *Soul, Body, and Survival: Essays on the Metaphysics of Human Persons* (Ithaca, NY: Cornell University Press, 2001), pp. 201–17.

— (ed.), *Soul, Body, and Survival: Essays on the Metaphysics of Human Persons* (Ithaca, NY: Cornell University Press, 2001).

Cortez, Marc, *Embodied Souls, Besouled Bodies: An Exercise in Christological Anthropology and Its Significance for the Mind/Body Debate* (London: T&T Clark, 2008).

Davis, Stephen T., "The Resurrection of the Dead," in Stephen T. Davis (ed.), *Death and Afterlife* (Basingstoke: Macmillan, 1989), pp. 119–44.

Dennett, Daniel, *Brainstorms: Philosophical Essays on Mind and Psychology* (Montgomery, VT: Bradford, 1978).

—, *Elbow Room: The Varieties of Free Will Worth Wanting* (Cambridge, MA: MIT Press, 1984).

—, "Natural Freedom," *Metaphilosophy* 36.4 (2005), pp. 449–59.

Eagly, Alice H., Anne E. Beall, and Robert J. Sternberg (eds), *The Psychology of Gender* (2nd ed., New York: Guilford, 2004).

Foster, John, "Psychophysical Causal Relations," *American Philosophical Quarterly* 5.1 (1968), pp. 64–70.

Gazzaniga, Michael S., *Nature's Mind: The Biological Roots of Thinking, Sexuality, Language and Intelligence* (New York: Basic, 1992).

Ginet, Carl, "Reasons Explanations of Action: Causalist versus Noncausalist Accounts," in Robert Kane (ed.), *The Oxford Handbook of Free Will* (Oxford: OUP, 2005), pp. 386–405.

Goetz, Stewart, "Modal Dualism: A Critique," in Kevin Corcoran (ed.), *Soul, Body, and Survival: Essays on the Metaphysics of Human Persons* (Ithaca, NY: Cornell University Press, 2001), pp. 89–104.

Gorman, Christine, and J. Madeleine Nash, "Sizing up the Sexes," *Time* 139.3 (1992), p. 42.

Gray, John, *Men Are from Mars, Women Are from Venus: A Practical Guide for Improving Communication and Getting What You Want in Your Relationships* (New York: HarperCollins, 1992).

Green, Joel B., "Eschatology and the Nature of Humans: A Reconsideration of Pertinent Biblical Evidence," *Science & Christian Belief* 14.1 (2002), p. 33.

Grenz, Stanley J., *The Social God and the Relational Self: A Trinitarian Theology of the Imago Dei* (Philadelphia: Westminster, 2001).

Grudem, Wayne A., *Systematic Theology: An Introduction to Biblical Doctrine* (Grand Rapids, MI: Zondervan, 1994).

Gundry, Robert H., *Soma in Biblical Theology, with Emphasis on Pauline Anthropology* (Cambridge: CUP, 1976).

Hampson, Elizabeth, and Scott D. Moffat, "The Psychobiology of Gender: Cognitive Effects of Reproductive Hormones in the Adult Nervous System," in Alice H. Eagly, Anne E. Beall, and Robert J. Sternberg (eds), *The Psychology of Gender* (2nd ed., New York: Guilford, 2004), pp. 38–64.

Harman, Allan M., "*Ezer*," in William A. VanGemeren (ed.), *New International Dictionary of New Testament Theology & Exegesis* (Grand Rapids, MI: Zondervan, 1998), pp. 378–79.

Hasker, William, *The Emergent Self* (Ithaca, NY: Cornell University Press, 1999).

—, *God, Time, and Knowledge* (Ithaca, NY: Cornell University Press, 1989).

—, "Swinburne's Modal Argument for Dualism: Epistemically Circular," *Faith and Philosophy* 15.3 (1998), pp. 366–70.

Heil, John, *Philosophy of Mind: A Guide and Anthology* (Oxford: OUP, 2004).

Hines, Melissa, "Androgen, Estrogen, and Gender: Contributions of the Early Hormone Environment to Gender-Related Behavior," in Alice H. Eagly, Anne E. Beall and Robert J. Sternberg (eds), *The Psychology of Gender* (2nd ed., New York: Guilford, 2004), pp. 9–37.

Hoekema, Anthony, *Created in God's Image* (Grand Rapids, MI: Eerdmans, 1986).

Hoffman, Joshua, and Gary S. Rosenkrantz, *Substance: Its Nature and Existence* (London New York: Routledge, 1997).

Irigaray, Luce, *An Ethics of Sexual Difference* (Ithaca, NY: Cornell University Press, 1993).

Jeeves, Malcolm. From Cells to Souls—and Beyond: Changing Portraits of Human Nature (Grand Rapids, MI: Eerdmans, 2004).

Jewett, Paul K., *Man as Male and Female: A Study in Sexual Relationships from a Theological Point of View* (Grand Rapids, MI: Eerdmans, 1975).

Jewett, Robert, *Paul's Anthropological Terms* (Leiden: Brill, 1971).

Kane, Robert, A Contemporary Introduction to Free Will (Oxford: OUP, 2005).

—, The Oxford Handbook of Free Will (Oxford: OUP, 2001).

Kim, Jaegwon, "Lonely Souls: Causality and Substance Dualism," in Kevin Corcoran (ed.), *Soul, Body, and Survival: Essays on the Metaphysics of Human Persons* (Ithaca, NY: Cornell University Press, 2001, pp. 30–43.

—, "The Mind–Body Problem after Fifty Years," *Royal Institute of Philosophy Supplement* 43 (1998), pp. 3–21.

Kripke, Saul A., "Identity and Necessity," in John Heil (ed.), *Philosophy of Mind: A Guide and Anthology*, pp. 128–33.

Larmer, Robert, "Mind–Body Interaction and the Conservation of Energy," *International Philosophical Quarterly* 26 (1986), pp. 277–85.

LeDoux, Joseph E., The Emotional Brain: The Mysterious Underpinnings of Emotional Life (New York: Simon & Schuster, 1996).

Levine, Joesph, "Materialism and Qualia: The Explanatory Gap," *Pacific Philosophical Quarterly* 64 (1983), pp. 354–415.

Lippa, Richard A., *Gender, Nature, and Nurture* (2nd ed., Mahwah, NJ: Lawrence Erlbaum Associates, 2005).

Looy, Heather, and Hessel III Bouma, "The Nature of Gender: Gender Identity in Persons Who Are Intersexed or Transgendered," *Journal of Psychology and Theology* 33.3 (2005), pp. 166–78.

MacIntyre, Alasdair C., *Whose Justice? Which Rationality?* (Notre Dame: University of Notre Dame Press, 1988).

Marecek, Jeanne, Mary Crawford, and Danielle Popp, "On the Construction of Gender, Sex, and Sexualities," in Alice H. Eagly, Anne E. Beall, and Robert J. Sternberg (eds), *The Psychology of Gender* (2nd ed., New York: Guilford, 2004), pp. 192–216.

McCann, Hugh, *The Works of Agency: On Human Action, Will, and Freedom* (Ithaca, NY: Cornell University Press, 1998).

McFarlane, Graham, Review of Niels Henrik Gregersen, *The Human Person in Science and Theology* (London: T&T Clark, 2000); *Science and Christian Belief* 14 (2002), pp. 94–95.

McKenna, Michael, "Compatibilism," in Edward N. Zalta (ed.), The Stanford Encyclopedia of Philosopy (Summer 2004 Edition) (accessed May 31, 2007; http://plato.stanford.edu/archives/fall2008/entries/compatibilism/).

Mele, Alfred R., and David Robb, "Rescuing Frankfurt-Style Cases," *Philosophical Review* 107 (1998), pp. 97–112.

Merricks, Trenton, "Endurance, Psychological Continuity, and the Importance of Personal Identity," *Philosophy and Phenomenological Research* 59 (1999), pp. 983–97.

—, "There Are No Criteria of Identity over Time," *Nous* 32 (1998), pp. 106–24.

Moir, Anne, and David Jessel, *Brain Sex: The Real Difference between Men and Women* (New York: Carol, 1991).

Moltmann, Jürgen, *Man: Christian Anthropology in the Conflicts of the Present* (trans. John Sturdy, London: SPCK, 1974).

Moreland, J. P., and Scott B. Rae, *Body and Soul: Human Nature and the Crisis in Ethics* (Downers Grove, IL: InterVarsity Press, 2000).

Murphy, Nancey, "The Resurrection Body and Personal Identity: Possibilities and Limits of Eschatological Knowledge," in Ted Peters, Robert J. Russell, and Michael Welker (eds), *Resurrection: Theological & Scientific Assessments* (Grand Rapids, MI: Eerdmans, 2002), pp. 202–18.

Nelson, James B., Embodiment: An Approach to Sexuality and Christian Theology (Minneapolis, MN: Augsburg, 1978).

Nicholson, L., "Interpreting Gender," *Signs* 20 (1994), pp. 79–105.

O'Connor, Timothy, Persons and Causes: The Metaphysics of Free Will (Oxford: OUP, 2000).

Osei-Bonsu, Joseph, "Anthropological Dualism in the New Testament," *Scottish Journal of Theology* 40.4 (1987), pp. 571–90.

Penrose, Roger, *The Emperor's New Mind* (Oxford: OUP, 1989).

Polanyi, Michael, *Personal Knowledge: Towards a Post-Critical Philosophy* (Chicago: University of Chicago Press, 1958).

Popper, Karl R., and John Carew Eccles, *The Self and Its Brain: An Argument for Interactionism* (New York: Springer International, 1977).

Rose, Steven P. R., "Introduction: The New Brain Sciences," in David A. Rees and Steven P. R. Rose (eds), *The New Brain Sciences: Perils and Prospects* (New York: CUP, 2004), pp. 3–14.

Sayers, Dorothy L., "The Human-not-Quite-Human," in *Are Women Human?* (Grand Rapids, MI: Eerdmans, 2005), pp. 51–69.

Schaffer, Jonathan, "The Metaphysics of Causation," in Edward N. Zalta (ed.), *The Stanford Encyclopedia of Philosophy* (Fall 2008 edition) (accessed March 24, 2009; http://plato.stanford.edu/archives/fall2008/entries/causation-metaphysics/).

Schwöbel, Christoph, "Human Being as Relational Being: Twelve Theses for a Christian Anthropology," in Christoph Schwöbel and Colin E. Gunton (eds), *Persons, Divine, and Human* (London: T&T Clark, 1991), pp. 141–65.

—, "Recovering Human Dignity," in R. Kendall Soulen and Linda Woodhead (eds), *God and Human Dignity* (Grand Rapids, MI: Eerdmans, 2006), pp. 44–59.

Searle, John R., *The Rediscovery of Mind* (Cambridge, MA: MIT Press, 1992).

Soulen, R. Kendall, and Linda Woodhead (eds), *God and Human Dignity* (Grand Rapids, MI: Eerdmans, 2006).

Stump, Eleanore, "Non-Cartesian Substance Dualism and Materialism without Reductionism," *Faith and Philosophy* 12 (1995), pp. 505–31.

Swinburne, Richard, *The Christian God* (Oxford: OUP, 1994).

Taliaferro, Charles, *Consciousness and the Mind of God* (Cambridge: CUP, 1994).

Tanner, Kathryn, "The Difference Theological Anthropology Makes," *Theology Today* 50.4 (1994), pp. 567–80.

Taylor, Charles, *Sources of the Self* (Cambridge: CUP, 1989).

Van Inwagen, Peter, *An Essay on Free Will* (New York: Clarendon, 1983).

—, "Possibility of Resurrection," *International Journal for Philosophy of Religion* 9.2 (1978), pp. 114–21.

VanLeeuwen, Mary Stewart, *My Brother's Keeper: What the Social Sciences Do (and Don't) Tell Us about Masculinity* (Downers Grove, IL: InterVarsity, 2002).

Warfield, Ted A., "Causal Determinism and Human Freedom Are Incompatible: A New Argument for Incompatibilism," *Philosophical Perspectives* 14 (2000), pp. 167–80.

Wolff, Hans Walter, *Anthropology of the Old Testament* (trans. Margaret Kohl, London: SCM, 1974).

World Council of Churches, *Christian Perspectives on Theological Anthropology: A Faith and Order Study Document* (Geneva: World Council of Churches, 2005).

SCRIPTURE INDEX

Genesis
1-2	12, 27
1-3	25-6
1.22	57
1.26-28	20, 21, 24, 30, 33
1.26	22
1.27-28	16, 24
1:27	14, 16, 25
1.28	57
1.31	34
2	23, 61
2.7	45
2.18	34
2.19-20	34
2.21-22	45
2.21-23	34
2.24-25	35
5.1-3	21
5.1	15
5.3	28
9.6	15, 16, 20
50.20	103

Exodus
20.4	32

Deuteronomy
30.15-19	114

Joshua
24.15	114

1 Kings
2:19-23	25

2 Kings
16.10	16

Job
1.6-2.6	25
2.29	103

Psalms
8.4-6	15
8.4	1
14.1-3	16
19.1	18
39.6	16
82	25
89.7	25
103.19	103
115.3	103
139.16	103

Proverbs
16.4	103
16.33	103

Ezekiel
1.5	16
1.10	16
1.13	16
14.6	114
24.14	114

SCRIPTURE INDEX

Isaiah		1 Corinthians	
6.1-8	25	11.7	15, 17
13.4	16	12.12-31	26
25.1	103	15.49	17
54.5	60		
		2 Corinthians	
Jeremiah		3.18	15, 17
7.1-15	114	4.4	15, 17
23.18	25		
		Ephesians	
Daniel		2.15	26
3	16	4.22-24	17
		4.24	15
Matthew		Eph. 5.25-32	60
3.2	114		
22.30	45, 61	Colossians	
		1.15	15, 32
John		2.9	32
1.1-18	26	3.3	8
1.32-33	26	3.10	17, 26
3.16-18	114		
5.17-29	26	Hebrews	
10.38	32	1.3	17
14-16	26	4.15	17
Acts		James	
2.23	103	3.9	15, 16,
4.27-28	103		17, 20
Romans		1 John	
1.19	18	3.2	8
1.20	28		
2.5-6	114	Revelation	
3.23	16	Rev. 21.2	60
8.29	17		

AUTHOR INDEX

Anderson, Ray S. 24n18
Aquinas, Thomas 18n7, 21n15
Aristotle 46n12
Atkins, Peter 78
Augustine 3, 57
Averill, Edward 78n22
Ayala, Francisco J. 20n10

Bailey, Derrick Sherwin 41
Baker, Lynne Rudder 82n33,
    89n46, 111n15, 121
Balswick, Jack O. 42
Balswick, Judith K. 42
Balthasar, Hans Urs von 5
Barash, David P. 48n18
Barr, James 23
Barth, Karl 5–6, 19, 24, 25, 26,
    36, 62
Beauvoir, Simone 46, 50
Berdyaev, Nikolai 45n7, 98
Berkouwer, G. C. 1, 5, 8, 9, 12–13
Bird, Phyllis A. 27
Black, C. Clifton 15
Bouma, Hessel 52n35, 56, 62
Braine, David 74n13
Brown, Warren S. 20n11
Brunner, Emil 46
Butler, Judith 52

Case-Winters, Anna 20n10
Churchland, Paul M. 71n5
Ciocchi, David M. 126
Cooper, John W. 73n9, 93n54
Corcoran, Kevin 89, 92

Cortez, Marc 38n39
Crawford, Mary 50

Davis, Stephen T. 96
Dennett, Daniel 91, 105, 124
Dickens, Charles 131

Eccles, John 78n24, 94n55
Edwards, Jonathan 104, 113
Eichrodt, Walther 93n52

Fausto-Sterling, Anne 51n28
Feinberg, John 112, 125
Fisher, Christopher L. 18n8, 20n10
Frame, John 104
Foster, John 76n18

Gazzaniga, Michael S. 21n14
Ginet, Carl 114n22
Goetz, Stuart 85n41, 94n55
Gonzalez, Michelle A. 56
Gorman, Christine 51n27
Gray, John 53n41
Green, Joel B. 93n53
Gregory of Nyssa 3, 45n6, 45n8,
    67n71
Grenz, Stanley J. 15n1, 16n5,
    20n13, 24n18, 28, 32n28, 37,
    47, 58, 64–6
Grudem, Wayne A. 49–50
Gundry, Robert H. 93n52

Hampson, Elizabeth 47n16, 51
Hansen, Carsten Marten 86

Hasker, William 73–4, 85n41,
    94n55, 96n57, 123n35
Helm, Paul 104, 113n19
Hines, Melissa 47, 47n16
Hoekema, Anthony 15
Hoffman, Joshua 76
Horton, Michael S. 33n30, 36

Inwagen, Peter van 83n34, 88,
    107n13
Irenaeus 3, 16n4, 18n6
Irigaray, Luce 59n56

Jeeves, Malcolm 71n6
Jenson, Robert 37
Jessel, David 48n18
Jewett, Paul 24n18, 25n20, 42,
    56, 62
Jewett, Robert 70n3, 93n52

Kane, Robert 102, 113n20,
    116–17
Keating, B. F. 78n22
Kim, Jaegwon 70n4, 76, 77, 80, 81
Kripke, Saul A. 89n45
Kümmel, Werner Georg 93n52

Larmer, Robert 78n23
Levin, Micael E. 83n34
Levine, Joseph 83n36
Lippa, Richard A. 48n19, 50,
    52n32, 54n45, 56
Lipton, Judith Eve 48n18,
Looy, Heather 52n35, 56, 62

MacDonald, Nathan 30, 36n35
Macquarrie, John 49n40
Marecek, Jeanne 50
Maximus 3
McFadyen, Alistair 25n20, 33, 34,
    63, 64
McFarlane, Graham 69n2
McCann, Hugh 114n22
McKenna, Robert 106n12

Merricks, Trenton 89n47, 90n48
Mikkola, Mari 50, 52n36
Milton, John 14
Moffat, Scott D. 47n16, 51
Moir, Anne 48n18
Moltmann, Jürgen 1, 2
Moreland, J. P. 71n7, 74, 94n55
Murphy, Nancey 90n48

Nash, J. Madeleine 51n27
Nelson, James B. 54–5, 66

O'Connor, Timothy 101n4,
    109, 121
Osei-Bonsu, Joseph 93n54

Pannenberg, Wolfhart 4, 5, 7
Penrose, Roger 79n26
Polanyi, Michael 114
Popp, Daniel 50
Popper, Karl 73n10, 78n24, 94n55

Rae, Scott 71n7, 74, 94n55
Rahner, Karl 5
Rolnick, Philip A. 15n1
Rosenkrantz, Gary S. 76

Sayers, Dorothy L. 53–4
Schaffer, Jonathan 125n39
Schwöbel, Christoph 3, 33n29,
    40n41, 56
Searle, John 82n32, 83
Shuster, Marguerite 24n18, 42,
    56, 62
Stoljar, Daniel 84n38
Stump, Eleonore 74
Swinburne, Richard 94n55,
    123n34

Taliaferro, Charles 75, 79n26,
    85n39, 94n55
Tanner, Kathryn 7, 24n18
Taylor, Charles 15n1
Tillich, Paul 5

AUTHOR INDEX

Van Huyssteen, Wentzel 20n10, 21n16

Van Leeuwen 47n15, 51n30, 52n37, 54n43, 54

Ware, Bruce 103n10, 112n16, 120

Warfield, Ted A. 125n37

Wolff, Hans Walter 70n3, 93n52

Wright, N. T. 93n54